Mapping Our World

Teacher's Guide

Unit 2

aw

aw says /aw/
Voiced

re-

means again
as in reread

Note: See New and Important Objectives on page 2 for a complete list of skills taught and reviewed.

Critical Foundations in Primary Reading

Marilyn Sprick, Ann Watanabe, Karen Akiyama-Paik, and Shelley V. Jones

A Cambium Learning® Company

BOSTON, MA • LONGMONT, CO

ISBN 13-digit: 978-1-60218-525-8
ISBN 10-digit: 1-60218-525-5

7 8 9 10 11 B&B 16 15 14 13 12

166852/6-12

Table of Contents

Unit 2

Mapping Our World

How to Teach the Lessons

End of the Unit

Read Well 2 Sequence and Sound Pronunciation Guide

Letter Sounds and Combinations

Cumulative Review of *Read Well 1* Sounds and Combinations (Ss, Ee, ee, Mm, Aa, Dd, th, Nn, Tt, Ww, Ii, Th, Hh, Cc, Rr, ea, sh, Sh, Kk, -ck, oo, ar, wh, Wh, ĕ, -y as in fly, Ll, Oo, Bb, all, Gg, Ff, Uu, er, oo as in book, Yy, a schwa, Pp, ay, Vv, Qq, Jj, Xx, or, Zz, a_e, -y as in baby, i_e, ou, ow as in cow, ch, Ch, ai, igh, o_e, ir) and:

Unit 2	Unit 3			Unit 5	Unit 6
aw /aw/ **Paw** Voiced	ew /o͞o/ **Crew** Voiced	ue /o͞o/ **Blue** Voiced	u_e /o͞o/ **Flute** Bossy E Voiced	ow /ōōō/ **Snow** Voiced (Long)	ge /j/ **Page** Voiced
Unit 6	**Unit 7**		**Unit 8**		**Unit 10**
-dge /j/ **Badge** Voiced	ci /sss/ **Circle** Unvoiced	ce /sss/ **Center** Unvoiced	kn /nnn/ **Knee** Voiced	ph /fff/ **Phone** Unvoiced	oa /ōōō/ **Boat** Voiced (Long)
Unit 11		**Unit 12**		**Unit 13**	
oi /oi/ **Point** Voiced	ea /ĕĕĕ/ **Bread** Voiced (Short)	gi /j/ **Giraffe** Voiced	au /au/ **Astronaut** Voiced	oy /oy/ **Boy** Voiced	

Affixes (including morphographs—affixes taught with meaning) and Open Syllables

Cumulative Review of *Read Well 1* Affixes (-ed, -en, -es, -ing, -ly, -s, -y, -tion) and:

Unit 2	Unit 3		Unit 5		Unit 6
re- **Means again** as in reread	un- **Means not** as in unhappy	ex- as in excited	o Open syllable /ō/ as in open and moment	-ful **Means full of** as in colorful	bi- **Means two** as in bicycle
Unit 7	**Unit 8**	**Unit 11**	**Unit 12**	**Unit 13**	
de- as in detective	-able as in comfortable	i Open syllable /ī/ as in silence and pilot	be- as in before	-ous as in enormous	dis- as in discover
Unit 14		**Unit 15**		**Unit 16**	
-al as in animal	-ible as in flexible	-or **Means one who** as in actor	-ment as in apartment	-ic as in scientific	pre- **Means before** as in preview
Unit 17		**Unit 18**		**Unit 19**	
-ity as in activity	-sion as in permission	-ness as in fairness	-less **Means without** as in helpless	in- as in insert	im- **Means not** as in impossible

Introduction
Mapping Our World

Story Notes

A Bird's-Eye View: Continue Maya and Ben's school experiences with "Mapping Our World." Mr. Chapman's students get carried away making maps of Earth, North America, the United States, their neighborhood, and home! Geography is fun from a bird's-eye view.

People on the Move: Why do people move? Each year, around 40 million Americans move—that's 3 out of 20 people. Odds are, many of your students will have moved at least once. These students will make connections with their packing experiences as they chant a little poem about "oodles and caboodles of jam-packed boxes."

Next, explore the history of moving. Immigration brings a wonderful mix of people and traditions from around the world. The end of the unit circles back to Maya as she shares a story from her personal history.

Recommended Read Alouds

The *Read Well 2* suggested Read Alouds enhance small group instruction—providing opportunities to further build background knowledge and vocabulary. Read Alouds should be read outside of time allocated for small group instruction.

There's a Map on My Lap! by Tish Rabe

Fiction • Narrative With Factual Content

The ever-popular Cat in the Hat provides a poetic introduction to maps—city maps, subway maps, marine charts, topographical maps, and more. Students also learn to use symbols, scales, compasses, and grids to make sense of maps.

Alexander, Who's Not (Do you hear me? I mean it!) Going to Move by Judith Viorst

Fiction • Realistic Narrative

Alexander's family is moving a thousand miles away, and he does not want to go. "Never. Not ever. No way. Uh, uh. N.O." Students will enjoy hearing how Alexander comes around to accepting the move.

Read Well Connections

There's a Map on My Lap adds insight into the maps Maya and Ben's class draw in "A Bird's-Eye View." *Alexander, Who's Not (Do you hear me? I mean it!) Going to Move* provides a child's perspective on moving and saying goodbye to familiar surroundings.

NOTE FROM THE AUTHORS

USING VOCABULARY

Read Well 2 is rich with vocabulary building. Keep a running list of vocabulary words on a bulletin board or chart. When you hear a student use the word, put his or her name by the word with a star.

New and Important Objectives

A Research-Based Reading Program

Phonemic Awareness
Phonics
Fluency
Vocabulary
Comprehension

Phonological and Phonemic Awareness

Segmenting; Blending; Rhyming; Onset and Rime;
Counting Syllables

Phonics

Cumulative Letter Sounds and Combinations

Review • Ss, Ee, ee, Mm, Aa, Dd, th, Nn, Tt, Ww, Ii, Th, Hh, Cc, Rr, ea, sh, Sh, Kk, -ck, oo, ar, wh, Wh, ĕ, -y (as in fly), Ll, Oo, Bb, all, Gg, Ff, Uu, er, oo (as in book), Yy, a (schwa), Pp, ay, Vv, Qq, Jj, Xx, or, Zz, a_e, -y (as in baby), i_e, ou, ow (as in cow), ch, Ch, ai, igh, o_e, ir

Cumulative Affixes and Morphographs

Review • -ed, -en, -er, -es, -est, -ing, -ly, -s, -y, -tion

★New Letter Sounds, Combinations, Affixes, Morphographs, and Related Words

aw (as in paw) • awesome, awful, claw, claws, crawl, dawn, drawing, drawings, law, lawn, paws, saw, seesaw, shawl, straw, yawn

re- • recount, redo, refill, replay, rewrite

★New Abbreviations

P.S., TV

★New Contractions

here's, weren't

★New Proper Nouns

Africa, Albert's, Alison, Andy, Asia, Betsy, Canada, Emily, Japan, Jason, Lopez, Mama, Mexico, Panama, Samoa, Spain, Wrights

★New Pattern Words

bath, bones, boxes, bunk, choose, clutch, clutching, count, counted, cram, crammed, dirt, drive, drool, drooling, faded, foot,

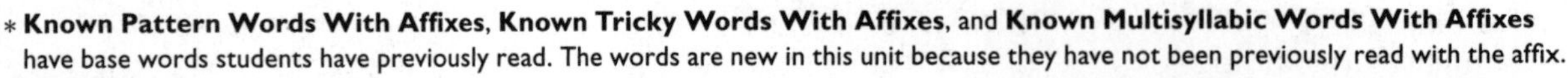

* **Known Pattern Words With Affixes**, **Known Tricky Words With Affixes**, and **Known Multisyllabic Words With Affixes** have base words students have previously read. The words are new in this unit because they have not been previously read with the affix.

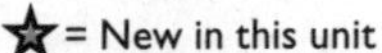

★= New in this unit

Phonics *(continued)*

fort, front, globe, house, least, looks, lunch, mail, mall, mine, most, nook, pen, piles, pinch, post, punch, rich, shape, shaped, share, shared, shirt, skates, slave, sort, spend, squeeze, stain, stained, stole, stolen, stomp, strip, takes, taste, these, tight, trade, traders, vast, wooden, woolen, wrap, write, writing, wrote

*__Known Pattern Words With Affixes__ • bikes, blocks, boxes, carefully, chairs, couches, floors, foods, girls, homes, hummed, missed, packing, parts, shocking, stacks, weeks, winning

☆New Compound and Hyphenated Words

a-okay, anyone, became, bedroom, bird's-eye, cowboy, e-mail, grandparents, herself, jam-packed, neighborhood, neighborhoods, suitcases, upstairs

☆Other New Multisyllabic Words

absolutely, action, attention, bandana, behind, belonging, belongings, birthday, button, caboodles, cattle, children, corner, customs, exists, immigrant, immigrants, immigrate, immigrating, involve, kitchen, offer, offered, oodles, parents, pebble, pretend, probably, purple, questions, readers, relative, relatives, snazzy, tasty, tradition, traditions, wagons, yummy

*__Known Multisyllabic Words With Affixes__ • bestest, families, muttering, stories

☆New Tricky Words

adventure, answer, areas, bear, been, boat, brought, busy, clothes, color, colorful, dino, dozens, earliest, early, face, favorite, few, goal, language, languages, million, new, nothing, nothing's, ocean, place, places, poem, sentence, sentences, show, slowly, spaces, super, sure, tables, true, truly, view, walk, wherever, women, wonder, wonderful

*__Known Tricky Words With Affixes__ • boys, countries, greats, ideas, moving, pictures, scientists, yours

Fluency

Accuracy, Expression, Phrasing, Rate

Vocabulary

New • belongings, continent, cram, globe, immigrant, neighborhood, planet, relative, tradition, vast

Review • bittersweet, inventor, perfect, pout

Reviewed in Context • perfect, plain

Idioms and Expressions

New • bird's-eye view

Review • get carried away

Comprehension

Unit Genres

Nonfiction • Expository
Fiction • Realistic Narrative, Imaginative Narrative

Comprehension Processes

Build Knowledge: Factual, Procedural, Conceptual

Day	1	2	3	4	5	6
Remember						
Defining						
Identifying (recalling)	S,C	E,S,C	E,S,C	C	S,C	
Using	S					
Understand						
Defining (in your own words)	S,C	S	S,C	S,C	S,C	
Describing		S	S	S	C	C
Explaining (rephrasing)	S	S	S,C	S,C		S
Illustrating		C	C	C		
Sequencing						
Summarizing						
Using	S,C	S	S,C	S,C	S,C	
Visualizing	S	C	S,C	C		
Apply						
Demonstrating	S					
Explaining (unstated)	S	S	S	S	S	S
Illustrating	C	C				
Inferring	S	S,C	S	S,C	S,C	
Making Connections (relating)	S		S,C	S	S	
Predicting	S					
Using	S	S,C	S	S	S	
Analyze						
Classifying		E,C		C		S
Comparing/Contrasting						
Distinguishing Cause/Effect						
Drawing Conclusions			E			
Inferring						
Evaluate						
Making Judgments					S	
Responding (personal)			C		C	
Create						
Generating Ideas			C	S		C

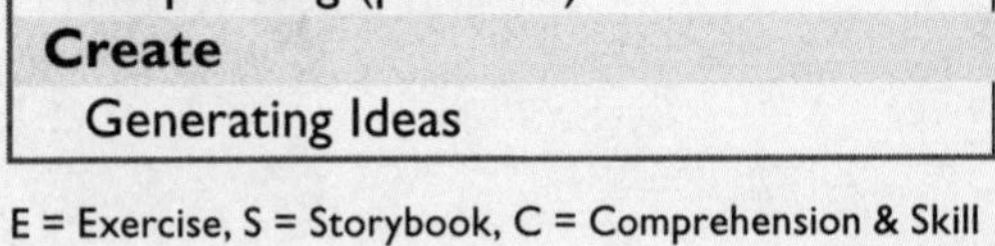

E = Exercise, S = Storybook, C = Comprehension & Skill

Comprehension *(continued)*

Skills and Strategies

Day	1	2	3	4	5	6
Priming Background Knowledge						
Setting a Purpose for Reading						
Answering Questions	S	S	S	S	S	S
Asking Questions						
Visualizing	S	C	S,C	C		
Comprehension Monitoring/Fix Ups						
Does it Make Sense?						C
Looking Back				C		
Restating						
Summarizing						
Main Idea		E,C		C		
Retelling						
Supporting Details						
Understanding Text Structure						
Title, Author, Illustrator	S	S	S	S	S	
Fact or Fiction						
Genre (Classifying)						S
Narrative						
Setting						
Main Character/Traits (Characterization)			E		C	C
Goal						
Problem/Solution						
Action/Events/Sequence		E				
Outcome/Conclusion						
Lesson/Author's Message						
Expository						
Subject/Topic		C	C			
Heading						
Supporting Details (Facts/Information)		S	C	C		
Main Idea				C		
Using Graphic Organizers						
Chart						
Diagram (labeling)						
Hierarchy (topic/detail)						
K-W-L						
Map (locating, labeling)	C	C				
Matrix (compare/contrast)						
Sequence (linear, cycle, cause and effect)						
Story Map						
Web		E	E		C	C

E = Exercise, S = Storybook, C = Comprehension & Skill

Comprehension *(continued)*

Study Skills

Day	1	2	3	4	5	6
Alphabetical Order			C			
Following Directions						C
Locating Information	S,C		S,C			C
Note Taking						
Previewing						
Reviewing		S			S	
Test Taking						
Using Glossary						
Using Table of Contents	S					C
Viewing						
Verifying						

Writing in Response to Reading

Day	1	2	3	4	5	6
Sentence Completion			C	C	C	C
Making Lists			C	C		
Sentence Writing		C		C	C	C
Story Retell/Summary						
Fact Summary						
Paragraph Writing						
Report Writing						
Open-Ended Response						
Creative Writing						

Writing Traits

(Addressed within the context of Writing in Response to Reading)

Day	1	2	3	4	5	6
Ideas and Content						
Elaborating/Generating						
Organization						
Introduction						
Topic Sentence						
Supporting Details						
Sequencing						
Word Choice						
Sophisticated Words (Tier 2 and 3)						
Conventions						
Capital		C	C	C	C	C
Ending Punctuation		C	C	C	C	C
Other (commas, quotation marks)						
Presentation						
Handwriting						C
Neatness						C

E = Exercise, S = Storybook, C = Comprehension & Skill

Daily Lesson Planning

LESSON PLAN FORMAT

Teacher-Directed 45 Minutes		Independent Teacher-Directed, as needed
Lesson Part 1 (Phonological Awareness, Phonics, Fluency, Comprehension) 15–20 Minutes	**Lesson Part 2** (Vocabulary, Fluency, Comprehension) 20–25 Minutes	**Lesson Part 3** (Vocabulary, Fluency, Comprehension) 15–20 Minutes
• Exercises	• Unit and/or Story Opener • Vocabulary • Interactive Story Reading • Short Passage Practice Timed Readings	• Story Reading With Partner or Whisper Reading • Comprehension and Skill Activities

HOMEWORK

Read Well 2 Homework (blackline masters of new *Read Well 2* passages) provides an opportunity for children to celebrate accomplishments with parents. Homework should be sent home on routine days.

ORAL READING FLUENCY ASSESSMENT

Upon completion of this unit, assess each student and proceed to Unit 3, as appropriate.

PACING REMINDER

There is no substitute for time. Most groups can complete this unit on a 6-Day Plan if sufficient amounts of time are allocated to instruction and independent work. Without sufficient time, students will not be able to master the content taught and may fail to achieve at an appropriate rate.

DIFFERENTIATED LESSON PLANS

The differentiated lesson plans illustrate how materials can be used for students with various learning needs. As you set up your unit plan, always include *Read Well 2* Exercises and Story Reading on a daily basis. Unit 2 includes 6-, 8-, 9-, 10-, and 11-Day Plans.

Plans	For groups that:
6-DAY	Complete Oral Reading Fluency Assessments with Passes and Strong Passes
8-DAY	Complete Oral Reading Fluency Assessments with Passes and require teacher-guided assistance with Story Reading and Comprehension and Skill Work
9-, 10-, or 11-DAY	Have difficulty passing the unit Oral Reading Fluency Assessments

6-DAY PLAN		
Day 1 **Teacher-Directed** • Exercise 1 • Unit and Story Opener: Mapping Our World, A Bird's-Eye View • Vocabulary, Ch. 1, 2 • A Bird's-Eye View, Ch. 1 • Guide practice, as needed, on Comp & Skill 1, 2 **Independent Work** • Repeated Reading: Whisper Read, A Bird's-Eye View, Ch. 1 • Comp & Skill 1, 2 **Homework** • Homework Passage 1	**Day 2** **Teacher-Directed** • Exercise 2a • Exercise 2b: Focus Lesson • A Bird's-Eye View, Ch. 2 • Guide practice, as needed, on Comp & Skill 3, 4 **Independent Work** • Repeated Reading: Whisper Read, A Bird's-Eye View, Ch. 2 • Comp & Skill 3, 4 **Homework** • Homework Passage 2	**Day 3** **Teacher-Directed** • Exercise 3a • Exercise 3b: Focus Lesson • Story Opener: People on the Move • Vocabulary, Ch. 1, 2 • People on the Move, Ch. 1 • Guide practice, as needed, on Comp & Skill 5, 6 **Independent Work** • Repeated Reading: Whisper Read, People on the Move, Ch. 1 • Comp & Skill 5, 6 **Homework** • Homework Passage 3
Day 4 **Teacher-Directed** • Exercise 4 • People on the Move, Ch. 2 • Guide practice, as needed, on Comp & Skill 7, 8 **Independent Work** • Repeated Reading: Whisper Read, People on the Move, Ch. 2 • Comp & Skill 7, 8 **Homework** • Homework Passage 4	**Day 5** **Teacher-Directed** • Exercise 5 • People on the Move, Ch. 3 • Guide practice, as needed, on Comp & Skill 9, 10 **Independent Work** • Repeated Reading: Whisper Read, People on the Move, Ch. 3 • Comp & Skill 9, 10 **Homework** • Homework Passage 5	**Day 6** **Teacher-Directed** • Exercise 6 • Fluency, That Kind of Day • Guide practice, as needed, on Comp & Skill 11, 12 **Independent Work** • Repeated Reading: Whisper Read, That Kind of Day • Comp & Skill 11, 12 • Oral Reading Fluency Assessment **Homework** • Homework Passage 6

Note: The 8-Day plan outlined on page 9 includes a day of review after "A Bird's-Eye View" and another day of review after "People on the Move." The sample plans offer a balanced selection of activities—a warm-up that includes repeated readings of previous stories, an exercise to review and build automaticity with decoding skills, and a time to check and correct selected Comprehension and Skill Activities or items.

<table>
<tr><th colspan="4">8-DAY PLAN • Pre-Intervention</th></tr>
<tr>
<td>Day 1
Teacher-Directed
• Exercise 1
• Unit and Story Opener: Mapping Our World, A Bird's-Eye View
• Vocabulary, Ch. 1, 2
• A Bird's-Eye View, Ch. 1
• Guide practice, as needed, on Comp & Skill 1, 2
Independent Work
• Repeated Reading: Whisper Read, A Bird's-Eye View, Ch. 1
• Comp & Skill 1, 2
Homework
• Homework Passage 1</td>
<td>Day 2
Teacher-Directed
• Exercise 2a
• Exercise 2b: Focus Lesson
• A Bird's-Eye View, Ch. 2
• Guide practice, as needed, on Comp & Skill 3, 4
Independent Work
• Repeated Reading: Whisper Read, A Bird's-Eye View, Ch. 2
• Comp & Skill 3, 4
Homework
• Homework Passage 2</td>
<td>Day 3 • Review
Warm-Up
• Repeated Reading: Whisper Read, A Bird's-Eye View, Ch. 1, 2 and Individual Timings
Teacher-Directed
• Review Exercise 1
• Repeated Reading: A Bird's-Eye View, Ch. 1, 2
• Check and correct Comp & Skill 1–4 (selected tasks)
Independent Work
• Correct and complete Comp & Skill 1–4
Homework
• Comp and Skill Activity 2 (Passage Fluency)</td>
<td>Day 4
Teacher-Directed
• Exercise 3a
• Exercise 3b: Focus Lesson
• Story Opener: People on the Move
• Vocabulary, Ch. 1, 2
• People on the Move, Ch. 1
• Guide practice, as needed, on Comp & Skill 5, 6
Independent Work
• Repeated Reading: Whisper Read, People on the Move, Ch. 1
• Comp & Skill 5, 6
Homework
• Homework Passage 3</td>
</tr>
<tr>
<td>Day 5
Teacher-Directed
• Exercise 4
• People on the Move, Ch. 2
• Guide practice, as needed, on Comp & Skill 7, 8
Independent Work
• Repeated Reading: Whisper Read, People on the Move, Ch. 2
• Comp & Skill 7, 8
Homework
• Homework Passage 4</td>
<td>Day 6
Teacher-Directed
• Exercise 5
• People on the Move, Ch. 3
• Guide practice, as needed, on Comp & Skill 9, 10
Independent Work
• Repeated Reading: Whisper Read, People on the Move, Ch. 3
• Comp & Skill 9, 10
Homework
• Homework Passage 5</td>
<td>Day 7 • Review
Warm-Up
• Repeated Reading: Whisper Read, People on the Move and Individual Timings
Teacher-Directed
• Review Exercise 3
• Repeated Reading: People on the Move
• Check and correct Comp & Skill 5–10 (selected tasks)
Independent Work
• Correct and complete Comp & Skill 5–10
Homework
• Repeat a selected Homework Passage</td>
<td>Day 8
Teacher-Directed
• Exercise 6
• Fluency, That Kind of Day
• Guide practice, as needed, on Comp & Skill 11, 12
Independent Work
• Repeated Reading: Whisper Read, That Kind of Day
• Comp & Skill 11, 12
• Oral Reading Fluency Assessment
Homework
• Homework Passage 6</td>
</tr>
</table>

<table>
<tr><th colspan="3">9-, 10-, or 11-DAY PLAN • Intervention
For Days 1–8, follow 8-Day plan. Add Days 9, 10, 11 as follows:</th></tr>
<tr>
<td>Day 9 Extra Practice 1
Teacher-Directed
• Decoding Practice
• Fluency Passage
Independent Work
• Activity and Word Fluency A
Homework
• Fluency Passage</td>
<td>Day 10 Extra Practice 2
Teacher-Directed
• Decoding Practice
• Fluency Passage
Independent Work
• Activity and Word Fluency B
Homework
• Fluency Passage</td>
<td>Day 11 Extra Practice 3
Teacher-Directed
• Decoding Practice
• Fluency Passage
Independent Work
• Activity and Word Fluency A or B
• Oral Reading Fluency Assessment
Homework
• Fluency Passage</td>
</tr>
</table>

Materials and Materials Preparation

Core Lessons

Teacher Materials

READ WELL 2 **MATERIALS**

- Unit 2 Teacher's Guide
- Sound Cards
- Unit 2 Oral Reading Fluency Assessment found on page 81
- Group Assessment Record found in the *Assessment Manual*

SCHOOL SUPPLIES

Stopwatch or watch with a second hand

Student Materials

READ WELL 2 **MATERIALS (for each student)**

- *Our World, Our Home* storybook
- *Exercise Book 1*
- *Activity Book 1* or copies of Unit 2 Comprehension and Skill Work
- Unit 2 Certificate of Achievement/Goal Setting (BLM, page 82)
- Unit 2 Homework (blackline masters)
  See *Getting Started* for suggested homework routines.

SCHOOL SUPPLIES

Pencils, colors (optional—markers, crayons, or colored pencils)

Make one copy per student of each blackline master, as appropriate for the group.

Note: For new or difficult Comprehension and Skill Activities, make overhead transparencies from the blackline masters. Use the transparencies to demonstrate and guide practice.

FOCUS LESSONS

For Exercises 2b and 3b (Focus Lessons), make overhead transparencies from the blackline masters, write on transparencies placed over the pages, or use paper copies to demonstrate how to complete the lessons.

Extra Practice Lessons

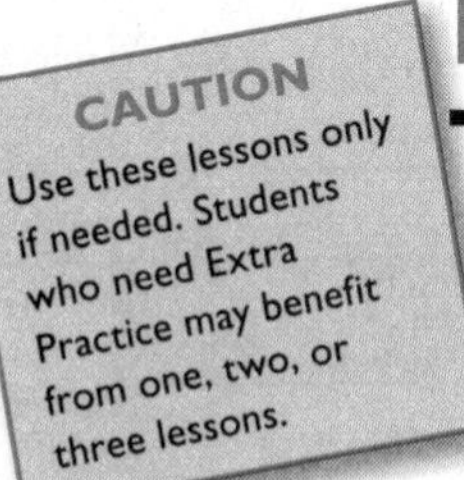

Student Materials

READ WELL 2 **MATERIALS (for each student, as needed)**

See Extra Practice blackline masters located on the CD.

- Unit 2 Extra Practice 1: Decoding Practice, Fluency Passage, Word Fluency A, and Activity
- Unit 2 Extra Practice 2: Decoding Practice, Fluency Passage, Word Fluency B, and Activity
- Unit 2 Extra Practice 3: Decoding Practice, Fluency Passage, Word Fluency A or B, and Activity

SCHOOL SUPPLIES

Pencils, colors (markers, crayons, or colored pencils), highlighters

Important Tips

When There's a Range in the Group

FLUENCY

Fluent reading is characteristic of a reader who is free of the word identification problems that often hinder comprehension. Fluency is "the ability to read a text quickly, accurately, and with proper expression" (National Reading Panel, 2000, p. 3-1). As students master the decoding process, many gradually develop fluency with ease, while others require focused practice.

MORE PRACTICE FOR SOME, NOT ALL

Even when students are carefully placed in small groups, individuals have varied practice needs. Because individuals need different amounts of practice, it is not uncommon to see a split in groups.

MINIMIZING THE RANGE: RULES OF THUMB

Watch carefully. If a split appears in your group or if an individual student is experiencing difficulty, act quickly.

FIRST RULE OF THUMB

A student who reads less fluently than the rest of the group requires more practice than other students.

SECOND RULE OF THUMB

When all students receive the same amount of practice, the gap between the highest- and the lowest-performing students will slowly become larger. To close this gap, you must increase practice opportunities for students with lower fluency rates.

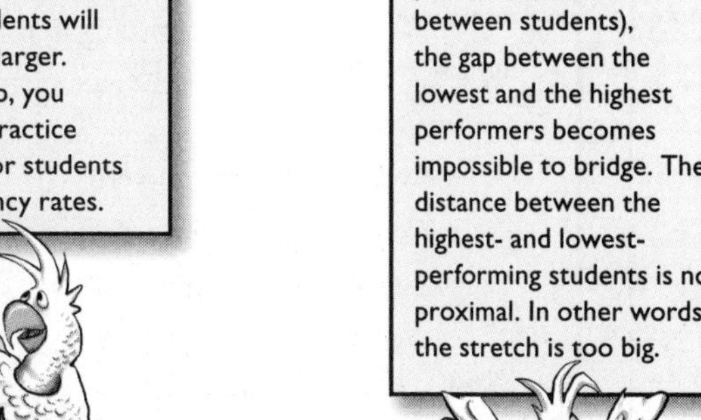

THIRD RULE OF THUMB

If the range in oral reading fluency rates becomes too large (e.g., a 20–30 word per minute difference between students), the gap between the lowest and the highest performers becomes impossible to bridge. The distance between the highest- and lowest-performing students is not proximal. In other words, the stretch is too big.

ACTION • OPTIONS FOR PRETEACHING AND REVIEW

1. Provide *more* practice for the lowest-performing students in a group. Be creative.
   - Have the lowest performers read their homework to other students before going home or first thing in the morning. (This may be in addition to reading at home or as a solution if a student has not been successful at doing his or her homework.)
   - Add Decoding Practice to the *Read Well* story reading homework. Use the Extra Practice Word Fluencies and Decoding blackline masters.
   - Set up extra reading opportunities. Have the student practice the day's Exercise with other students while others in the class line up for recess.
   - Parents who pick up their children from school often arrive a few minutes early. Ask these parents to listen to a student reread his or her story or Exercise while the class is cleaning up for the day.

2. Divide your reading block so that the lowest performers review or preview the units and receive more teacher-directed time. For example, if you have a 60-minute reading block with one group, divide your time as follows:
   - 10 minutes: Exercise preview with low-fluency students while other students do Partner Reading and work on handwriting fluency.
   - 30–35 minutes: Exercise and Story Reading with all students in the group.
   - 15–20 minutes: Comprehension and Skill Work with all students in the group.
     One by one, have low-fluency students reread the story one-to-one with the teacher (Short Passage Practice and a one-minute timing).

ACTION • GOAL SETTING

The lowest students in any group sometimes feel that they are helpless. These students may not understand that there is a cause-effect relationship between what they do and their reading fluency. Actively teach students that what they do makes a difference. Use goal setting to help them take action. Use one of the many goal-setting forms provided periodically in the End of the Unit section of the teacher's guides.

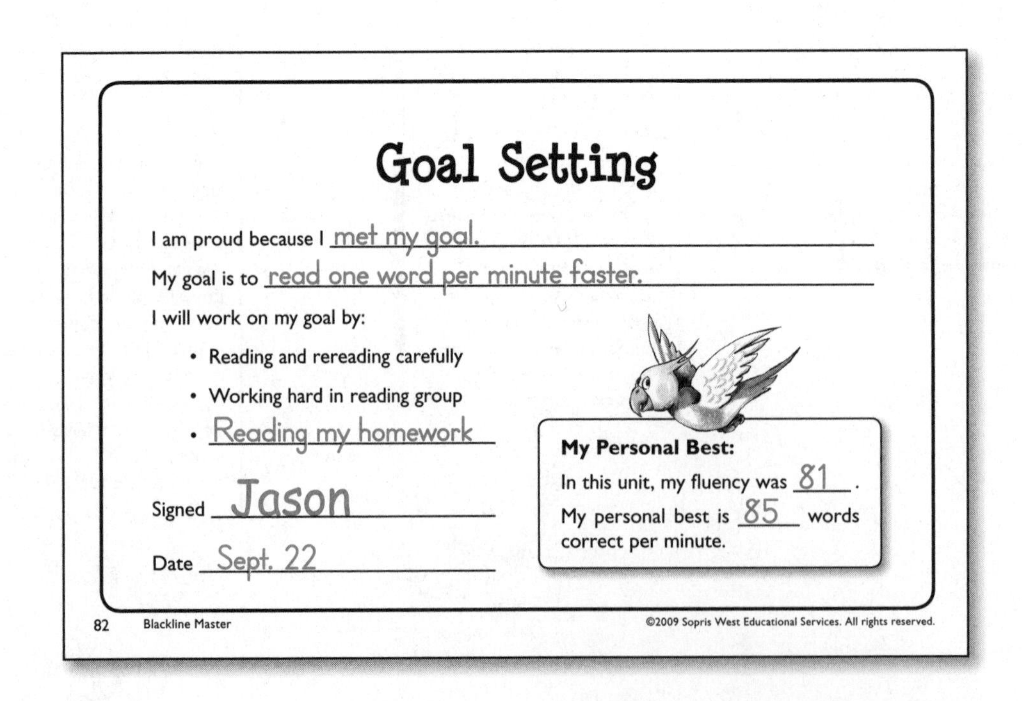

Goal Setting

I am proud because I met my goal.

My goal is to read one word per minute faster.

I will work on my goal by:

- Reading and rereading carefully
- Working hard in reading group
- Reading my homework

Signed Jason

Date Sept. 22

My Personal Best:

In this unit, my fluency was 81.

My personal best is 85 words correct per minute.

82 Blackline Master

©2009 Sopris West Educational Services. All rights reserved.

How to Teach the Lessons

Teach from this section. Each instructional component is outlined in an easy-to-teach format.

Exercise 1

- Unit and Story Opener: Mapping Our World, A Bird's-Eye View
- Vocabulary
- Story Reading 1
  With the Teacher: Chapter 1
- Comprehension and Skill Activities 1, 2

Exercise 2a

- Exercise 2b: Focus Lesson
- Story Reading 2
  With the Teacher: Chapter 2
- Comprehension and Skill Activities 3, 4

Exercise 3a

- Exercise 3b: Focus Lesson
- Story Opener: People on the Move
- Vocabulary
- Story Reading 3
  With the Teacher: Chapter 1
- Comprehension and Skill Activities 5, 6

Exercise 4

- Story Reading 4
  With the Teacher: Chapter 2
- Comprehension and Skill Activities 7, 8

Exercise 5

- Story Reading 5
  With the Teacher: Chapter 3
- Comprehension and Skill Activities 9, 10

Exercise 6

- Story Reading 6, Fluency
  With the Teacher: That Kind of Day
- Comprehension and Skill Activities 11, 12

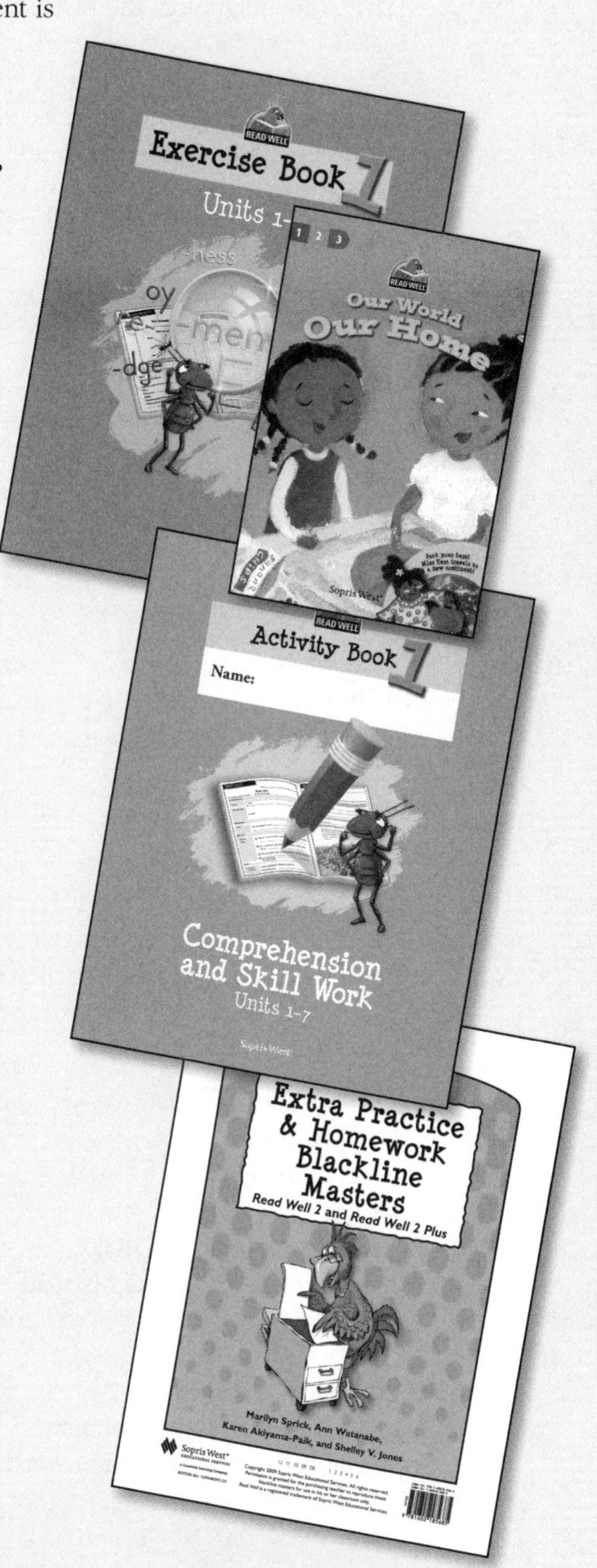

Note: Lessons include daily homework.

PACING
Exercise 1 should take about 15 minutes.

❶ SOUND REVIEW

Use selected Sound Cards from Unit 1.

★❷ NEW SOUND INTRODUCTION

- Tell students a-w says /aw/ as in paw.
- Have students look at the picture, identify "paw," and read the sentence.
  I saw a brown bear with big *paws* and sharp claws.
- Have students practice: a-w says /aw/ as in paw.
- Have students read the sentence again, then identify the three words with /aw/.
- For Rows B and C, have students read any underlined part, then the word.

❸ ACCURACY AND FLUENCY BUILDING

IMPORTANT PROCEDURES: ACCURACY AND FLUENCY BUILDING
For each task, have students say any underlined part, then read the word.
Set a pace. Then have students read the whole words in each task and column.
Provide repeated practice, building accuracy first, then fluency.

B1. Reading by Analogy

Have students figure out how to say *e-* and *o-* by reading other words they know.

D2. Story Words

Tell students the underlined sound, then have them read the word.

E1. Tricky Words

- For each Tricky Word, have students identify known sounds or word parts. Use the word in a sentence to help with pronunciation.
- If the word is unfamiliar, tell students the word. Then have students say, spell, and say it.

view
Look at the first word. The word is *view*. Say the word. (view)
I hiked to the top of the mountain. I had a great . . . *view*.
Spell *view*. (v-i-e-w)
Read the word three times. (view, view, view)

neighborhoods
Look at the next word. The first part is really tricky; it says "neigh."
Read the word by parts with me. neigh-bor-hoods
People who live near each other live in . . . *neighborhoods*.
Read the word three times. (neighborhoods, neighborhoods, neighborhoods)

eye	I can close one . . . *eye*.
million	When Ted grows up, he said he's going to earn a . . . *million* . . . dollars.
island	Hawaii is an . . . *island*.
country(ies)	America is a . . . *country*. America and Canada are . . . *countries*.

❹ MULTISYLLABIC WORDS

For each word, have students read each syllable, finger count, then read the whole word. Use the word in a sentence, as appropriate.

★❺ MORPHOGRAPHS

- Tell students that a morphograph is a word part that means something.

★Introduce "re = again." Say something like:
Morphographs are word parts that mean something.
Look at Row A. The morphograph *re-* means again. So we say that *re-* equals again.

★= New in this unit

Everyone read that with me. *Re-* equals again. Read the next phrase and then the sentence. (Redo equals do again. I want my project to be perfect. I will redo it.)

- Demonstrate and guide students in rephrasing the sentence.
  Another way to say "I will redo it" is "I will do it . . . again."
- Repeat for Rows B and C.

A Bird's-Eye View

Unit 2 Exercise 1

Use before Chapter 1

1. SOUND REVIEW Use selected Sound Cards from Unit 1.

★2. NEW SOUND INTRODUCTION Introduce the new sound /aw/ as in paw.

A	aw 	 paw	I saw a brown bear with big paws and sharp claws.	
B	law	yawn	crawl	draw
C	drawing	awful	seesaw	

3. ACCURACY AND FLUENCY BUILDING For each column, have students say any underlined part, then read each word. Next, have students read the whole column.

A1 Mixed Practice	B1 Reading by Analogy	C1 Word Endings	D1 Places	E1 Tricky Words
vast	me	seems	United States	view
snazzy	he	really	North America	neighborhoods
story	e-	shaped	Samoa	eye
parts	even	yours	Canada	million
flat		readers	Earth	island
A2 Bossy E	no	**C2** Buildups	**D2** Story Words	country
homes	go	all	show	countries
share	most	mall	place	world
states		small	boy	walk
globe		smaller	sentence	

4. MULTISYLLABIC WORDS Have students read and finger count each word part, then read each whole word.

A	per•fect	perfect	per•haps	perhaps
B	plan•et	planet	build•ing	building
C	con•ti•nent	continent	ev•ery•thing	everything

★5. MORPHOGRAPHS Have students practice reading "re = again" and the related words and sentences.

A★	re = again	redo = do again	I want my project to be perfect. I will redo it.
B		replay = play again	I missed the game on TV. I must see a replay.
C		refill = fill again	I drank my glass of water. I will get a refill.

8

TEAM EXPECTATIONS (Reminder)

Provide a quick review of expectations before starting the lesson.

1. Sit up.
2. Follow directions.
3. Help each other.
4. Work hard and have fun.

ACKNOWLEDGE STUDENTS WHEN THEY MEET YOUR EXPECTATIONS

Students respond positively when you acknowledge their accomplishments. Pair descriptive praise with an individual turn or job.

[Shelley], I like the way you have your finger under the right word. You get to read the row all by yourself. Everyone, follow the words with your fingers while [Shelley] reads.

COMPREHENSION PROCESSES

Remember, Understand, Apply

PROCEDURES

1. Introducing the Unit and Using the Table of Contents

Using Table of Contents; Identifying—Title; Locating Information

Have students turn to the Table of Contents on page 4.
Tell students the title of their new unit is "Mapping Our World."
Say something like:

Look at the Table of Contents on page 4.

We just finished reading Unit 1, "Maya and Ben."
Today, we're going to start Unit 2, "Mapping Our World."
What do you think you're going to learn about? (maps . . .)

This unit has two stories. The first one is called "A Bird's-Eye View."
What is the first story in Unit 2 called? (A Bird's-Eye View)
What page does "A Bird's-Eye View" begin on? (page 31)

What's the second story called? (People on the Move)
What page does "People on the Move" start on? (page 42)

2. Using the Title Page and Introducing the Story

Identifying—Title; Inferring; Visualizing; Defining and Using Idioms and Expressions—bird's-eye view

Have students turn to the title page. Introduce the story.

Turn to page 31. This is the title page.
What's the title of the story?
(A Bird's-Eye View)
That's an interesting title. Close your eyes.
Imagine that you are a bird flying above our school.
What would you see? (the top of the playground, the roof of our school . . .)
That's right. Open your eyes.
What a bird would see from above is called a . . . bird's-eye view.

TABLE OF CONTENTS

UNIT 2 • **Mapping Our World**

4

UNIT 2

Mapping Our World

30

A Bird's-Eye View

by Ms. Mak
illustrated by Jana Christy

Bird's-Eye View
Bird's-Eye View

Look at the picture. Imagine you are the bird flying over this neighborhood. What do you see below you?

31

MODEL ENTHUSIASM

To encourage students' interest in character or setting, think aloud. Model your enthusiasm. Say something like:

I'm excited about this story because you are going to learn about maps. Maps are great. We can use them to find where we live, where we might travel, and where things are happening in the world.

COMPREHENSION PROCESSES

Remember, Understand, Apply

PROCEDURES

Introducing Vocabulary

★ **planet** ★ **globe**
★ **continent**
★ **neighborhood** ★ **vast,**
get carried away

- For each vocabulary word, have students read the word by parts, then read the whole word.
- Read the student-friendly explanations to students as they follow with their fingers. Then have students use the vocabulary word by following the gray text.
- Review and discuss the photos and illustrations, as appropriate.

USING VOCABULARY

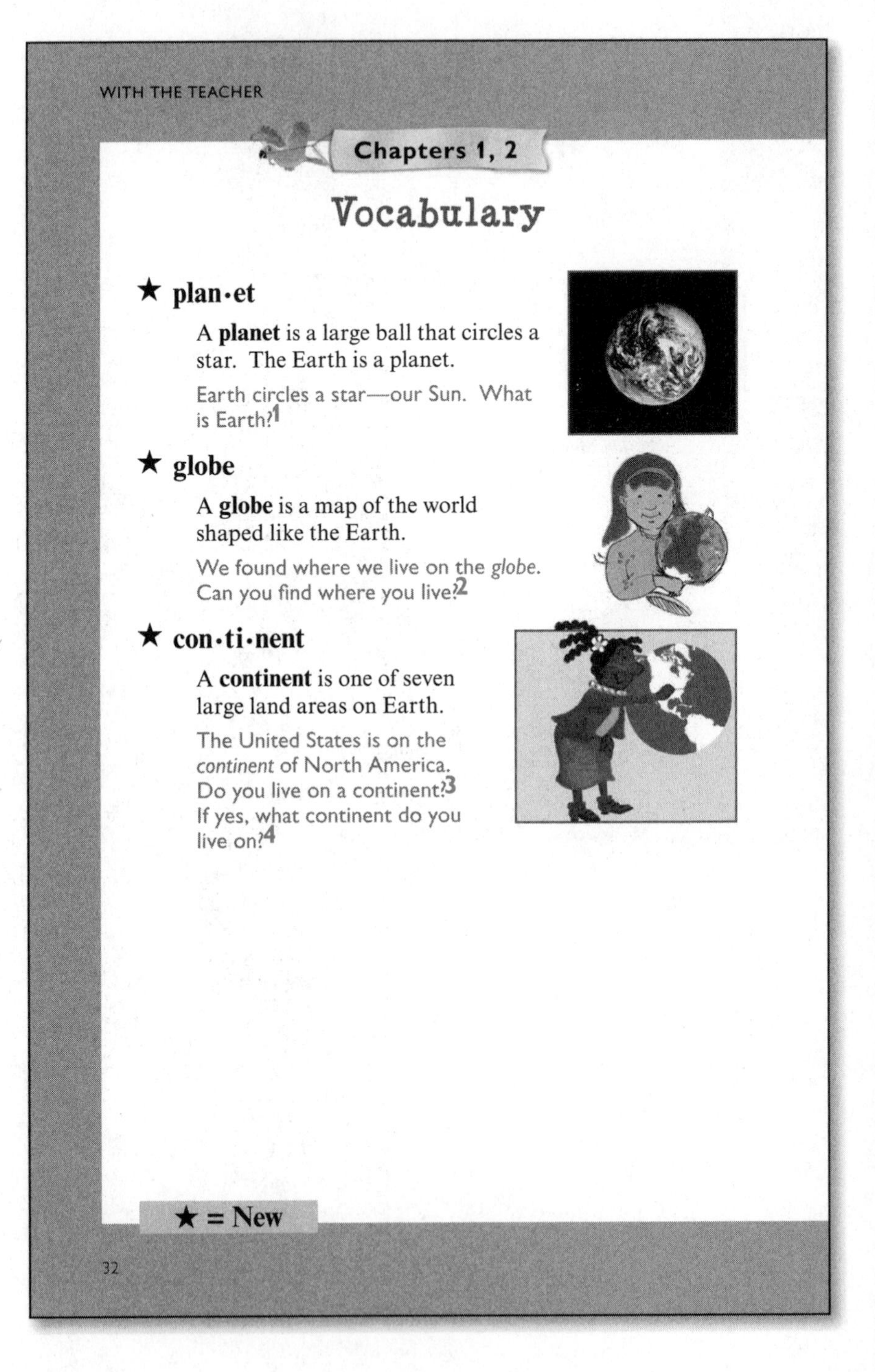

❶ **Remember:** Identifying—What; Using Vocabulary—planet (The Earth is a planet.)
❷ **Apply:** Using Vocabulary—globe; Demonstrating
❸ **Apply:** Using Vocabulary—continent ([yes])
❹ **Understand:** Identifying—What ([North America])

★ = New in this unit

★ **neigh•bor•hood**

A **neighborhood** is a part of a town. It is made up of people who live near each other.

Every *neighborhood* is different. This is my neighborhood. What's in your neighborhood?[1]

★ **vast**

A place that is **vast** is very great in size. It is enormous.

The ocean is enormous. It is . . .[2]

Idioms and Expressions

get car•ried a•way

If you **get carried away** with something, you do more than you had planned.

Maya, Ben, and Ana needed only one map for their project. How did you know they *got carried away* with their map project?[3]

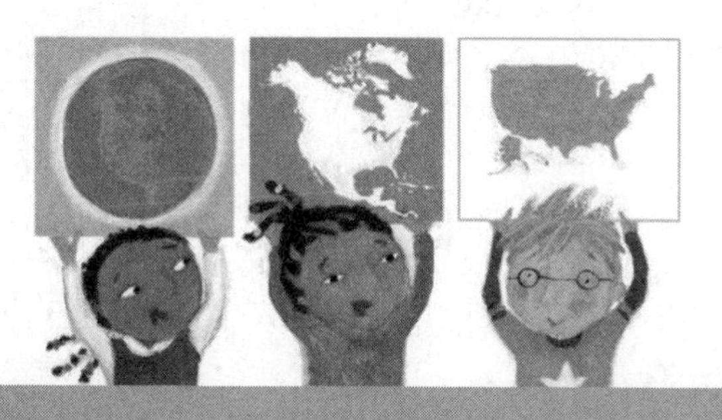

USING VOCABULARY

❶ **Understand:** Using Vocabulary—neighborhood (There are houses, stores, and trees in my neighborhood . . .)

❷ **Understand:** Using Vocabulary—vast (vast)

❸ **Apply:** Explaining, Using Idioms and Expressions—get carried away (They got carried away because they needed only one map, but they made many maps.)

CHAPTER 1 INSTRUCTIONS

Students read with the teacher.

COMPREHENSION PROCESSES

Remember, Understand, Apply

COMPREHENSION BUILDING

- Encourage students to answer questions with complete sentences.
- If students have difficulty comprehending, think aloud with them or reread the portion of the story that answers the question. Then ask the question again.

PROCEDURES

1. Introducing the Chapter

Identifying—Title; Predicting

Discuss the title. Say something like:

Read the title of the chapter. (Our World)

That's right. The first chapter of "A Bird's-Eye View" is called "Our World."

What do you think you are going to learn about?

2. First Reading

- Ask questions and discuss the story as indicated by the gray text.
- Mix group and individual turns, independent of your voice.
  Have students work toward a group accuracy goal of 0–4 errors.
  Quietly keep track of errors made by all students in the group.
- After reading the story, practice any difficult words.
  Reread the story if students have not reached the accuracy goal.

CORRECTING DECODING ERRORS

During story reading, gently correct any error, then have students reread the sentence.

3. Second Reading, Short Passage Practice: Developing Prosody

- Demonstrate expressive, fluent reading of the first paragraph.
  Read at a rate slightly faster than the students' rate. Say something like:
  In the first three paragraphs under the photo, the book provides us with factual information. We're going to read it like a professional narrator on a science show. Listen to me first.

  "Our Planet. Earth is my home and yours too. We all share the planet Earth. When we walk on Earth, everything seems flat. However, Earth is really round. A globe is a . . . "
- Guide practice with your voice.
- Provide individual turns while others finger track and whisper read.
  Provide descriptive, positive feedback.
  [Jeremy], you sounded just like a narrator on a *National Geographic* special!
- Repeat with one paragraph at a time.

PARTNER READING

Partner Reading procedures will be taught in Unit 3. If your students have been in *Read Well Fluency Foundations*, continue Partner or Whisper Reading procedures during independent work.

4. Whisper Reading: Repeated Reading

Have students finger track and whisper read before beginning independent work.

5. Homework 1: Repeated Reading

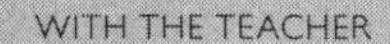

Our World

Our Planet

Earth is my home and yours too. We all share the planet Earth.

When we walk on Earth, everything seems flat. However, Earth is really round.

A globe is a round map shaped like the Earth. A globe is a great way to show what Earth looks like.

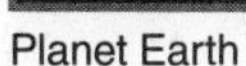

Planet Earth Globe

What is Earth?**1** What is a *globe*?**2**

34

MANAGEMENT TIP: FINGER TRACKING (Reminder)

To help students keep their places, pay attention, and practice while others read, continue to have students track text with their fingers. Provide positive feedback and individual turns to students who are finger tracking.

Say something like:
[Jason], You get a turn because you are following along.

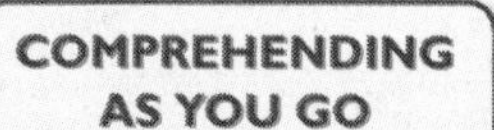

1. **Remember:** Identifying—What; Using Vocabulary—planet (Earth is a planet. Earth is our home.)
2. **Understand:** Defining and Using Vocabulary—globe (A globe is a round map shaped like the Earth.)

Most maps that we draw are flat maps. Most flat maps are drawings of smaller parts of the Earth—the continents, islands, countries, and states. We can draw maps of our neighborhoods, buildings, and even our homes.

Our Continents

Continents are vast areas of land. There are seven continents in the world. Most of you live on the continent of North America.

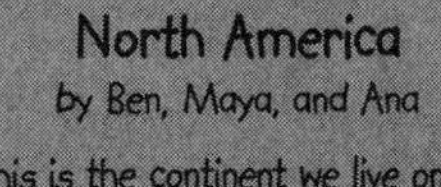

What is a *continent*?[1] What continent do Ben, Maya, and Ana live on?[2] Do you live on a continent or an island?[3]

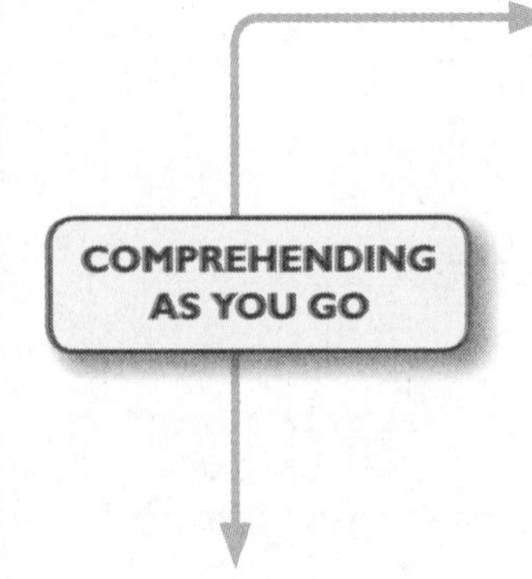

❶ **Understand:** Defining and Using Vocabulary—continent (A continent is vast. There are seven continents. They are big areas of land . . .)

❷ **Understand:** Explaining; Using Vocabulary—continent (They live on the continent of North America.)

❸ **Apply:** Making Connections (I live on [a continent].)

WITH THE TEACHER

Our Countries

A country can be big or small. There are about 192 countries in the world.

What country do you live in? Many of you live in the United States, but some of you may live in Canada, or perhaps even on the island country of Samoa.

You and other readers share the Earth and perhaps a continent and a country. Are we perfect or what?

Why does Maya think we are perfect?[1]

36

COMPREHENDING AS YOU GO

❶ **Apply:** Inferring; Explaining; Using Vocabulary—continent, neighborhood, perfect
(We are perfect because we all share the Earth, a continent, and a country. She thinks we are perfect because she is happy with her friends, her school, her neighborhood, her country, and the world.)

★PASSAGE COMPREHENSION

COMPREHENSION PROCESSES

Remember, Understand, Apply

Identifying—What
Using Vocabulary—planet

Identifying—What

Identifying—What
Using Vocabulary—continent

Identifying—What

Using Graphic Organizer
Illustrating; Defining and
Using Vocabulary—globe
Locating Information

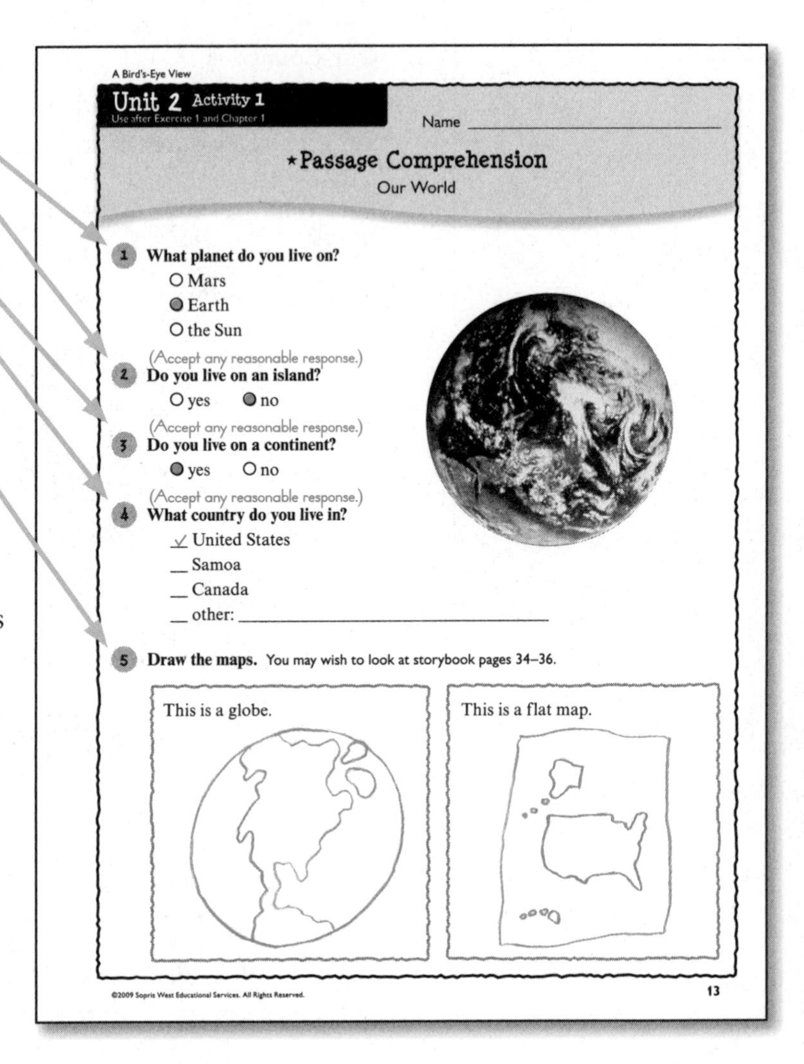

A Bird's-Eye View

Unit 2 Activity 1
Use after Exercise 1 and Chapter 1

Name ____________________

★Passage Comprehension
Our World

1. What planet do you live on?
   - ○ Mars
   - ● Earth
   - ○ the Sun

(Accept any reasonable response.)
2. Do you live on an island?
   ○ yes ● no

(Accept any reasonable response.)
3. Do you live on a continent?
   ● yes ○ no

(Accept any reasonable response.)
4. What country do you live in?
   - ✓ United States
   - __ Samoa
   - __ Canada
   - __ other: ____________________

5. Draw the maps. You may wish to look at storybook pages 34–36.

This is a globe.	This is a flat map.

13

PROCEDURES

For each step, demonstrate and guide practice, as needed. Then have students complete the page independently.

1. **Selection Response—Basic Instructions** (Items 1–4)
   Have students read each question, then fill in the bubble for or check the correct answer.
   Note: For Item 4, have students check the correct answer. If "other" is selected, have them fill in the country you live in.

★ 2. **Map: Illustrating—Introductory Instructions** (Item 5)

- Have students read item 5 and identify where they can look in their book for help.
  Find item 5. It says, "Draw the maps."
  Now read the small print with me. (You may wish to look at storybook pages 34 to 36.)
  Where can you look if you want to see how to draw a globe or map? (pages 34 to 36)
- Have students read the sentence in the first box and draw a globe. Say something like:
  We learned in our story that there are two types of maps.
  You're going to draw each type of map. Read the sentence in the first box. (This is a globe.)
  What is a globe? (a round map shaped like the Earth)
  To draw a globe, first you'll draw a circle, like this. **Draw a circle.**
  Next, we need to draw some of the continents and the oceans. I'm not sure how to do that.
  Where should I look? (pages 34 to 36)
  Let's do that. Raise your hand when you can find a drawing of a globe. [Tyrone], where did you find a picture of a globe? (page 35)
  Yes, there's a picture of a globe on Ben's poster. So I can copy what Ben drew.
- Repeat with the second box for a flat map.

★= New in this unit

PASSAGE READING FLUENCY

FLUENCY

Accuracy, Expression, Rate

PROCEDURES

For each step, demonstrate and guide practice, as needed. Then have students complete the page independently.

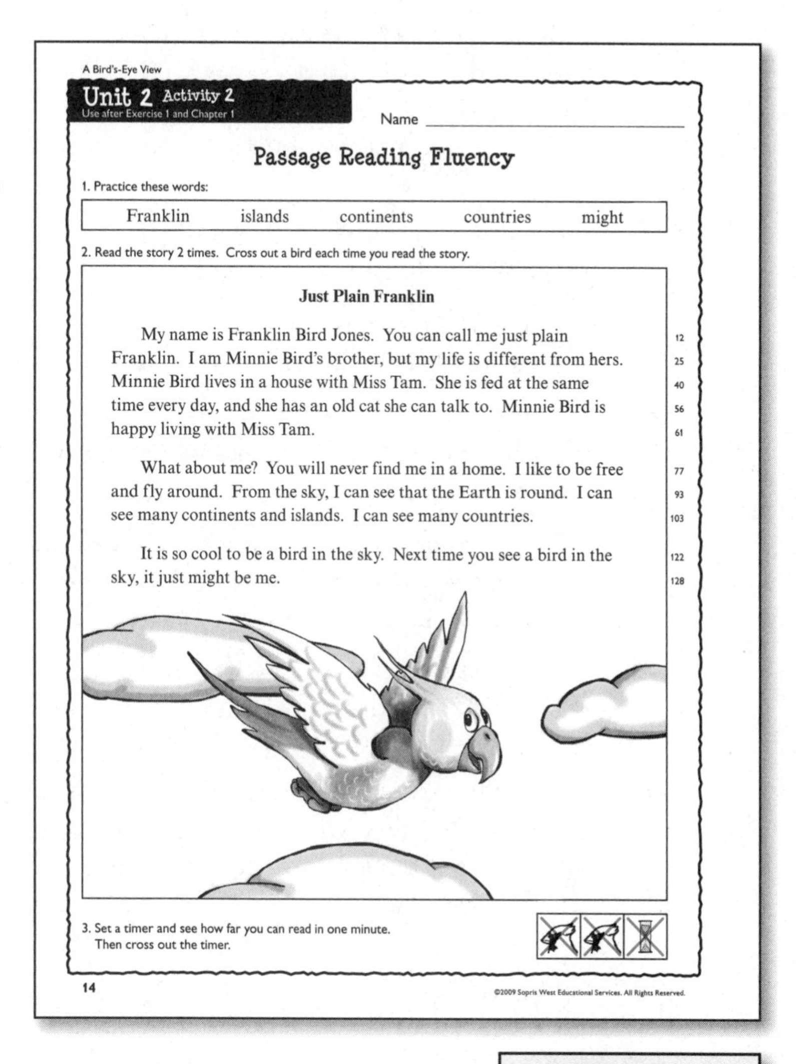

A Bird's-Eye View

Unit 2 Activity 2
Use after Exercise 1 and Chapter 1

Name ____________________

Passage Reading Fluency

1. Practice these words:

Franklin   islands   continents   countries   might

2. Read the story 2 times. Cross out a bird each time you read the story.

Just Plain Franklin

My name is Franklin Bird Jones. You can call me just plain Franklin. I am Minnie Bird's brother, but my life is different from hers. Minnie Bird lives in a house with Miss Tam. She is fed at the same time every day, and she has an old cat she can talk to. Minnie Bird is happy living with Miss Tam. 12 25 40 56 61

What about me? You will never find me in a home. I like to be free and fly around. From the sky, I can see that the Earth is round. I can see many continents and islands. I can see many countries. 77 93 103

It is so cool to be a bird in the sky. Next time you see a bird in the sky, it just might be me. 122 128

3. Set a timer and see how far you can read in one minute.
Then cross out the timer.

14

©2009 Sopris West Educational Services. All Rights Reserved.

Passage Reading—Basic Instructions

- Have students read the practice words.
- Have students finger track and whisper read the story two times—the first time for accuracy and the second for expression. Have students cross out a bird each time they finish.
- Have students do a one-minute Timed Reading. Have students cross out the timer when they finish. Say something like:

  You are going to track with your finger and whisper read.

  You are going to read the passage three times.

  The first time, read for accuracy. What will you read for? (accuracy)

  The second time, read for accuracy and expression.

  What will you read for? (accuracy and expression)

  Each time you read, cross out a bird and notice how much better your reading sounds. The last time you read, use the timer. Read quickly, but accurately and with expression. See if you can finish reading before one minute is up.

ACCURACY PRECEDES RATE (Reminder)

Students should read the story with a high degree of accuracy before proceeding to Timed Readings. Reading for increased rate before establishing a high degree of accuracy may encourage students to guess at words.

❶ SOUND REVIEW

Use selected Sound Cards from Units 1 and 2.

PACING
Exercises 2a and 2b should take about 20 minutes.

❷ ACCURACY AND FLUENCY BUILDING

- For each task, have students say any underlined part, then read the word.
- Set a pace. Then have students read the whole words in each task and column.
- Provide repeated practice, building accuracy first, then fluency.

B1. Bossy E

For each word, have students identify the Bossy E on the end of the word. Have students identify the underlined sound and then read the word.

C1, D2. Rhyming Words

Have students read each set. Ask students how each set of words is the same.

★D1. Possessives

- Tell students that words ending with an apostrophe s own something. Say something like: If a word ends with an apostrophe s, something belongs to it.
- Have students read each word. Guide students as they identify what is owned. Read the first word. (Albert's) Albert's dog is big. What belongs to Albert? (a dog) Repeat with each word.

  For the word "kids'," say something like: The word *kids'* ends with an s apostrophe. That means that more than one kid owns something. The four kids' shirts were all dirty. What belongs to the four kids? (shirts)

E1. Tricky Words

- For each Tricky Word, have students identify known sounds or word parts. Use the word in a sentence to help with pronunciation.
- If the word is unfamiliar, tell students the word. Then have students say, spell, and say it.

been

Try to sound out the first Tricky Word in your head.
Thumbs up when you know the word. Use my sentence to help you pronounce the word.
My mother asked, "Where have you . . . *been?*" Spell *been.* (b-e-e-n)
Read the word five times. (been, been, been, been, been)

Martinez

Look at the next word. It's a last name. The word is *Martinez.* Say the word. (Martinez)
Her name is Maya . . . *Martinez.* Read the word three times. (Martinez, Martinez, Martinez)

E2. Story Words

Tell students the underlined sound, then have them read the word.

❸ COMPOUND WORDS

For each word, have students read each small word, then read the compound word.

❹ MULTISYLLABIC WORDS

For each word, have students read each syllable, finger count, then read the whole word. Use the word in a sentence, as appropriate.

★= New in this unit

5 MORPHOGRAPHS

Have students read "re = again" and the related words and sentences, then rephrase each sentence.

A Bird's-Eye View

Unit 2 Exercise 2a

Use before Exercise 2b (Focus Lesson)

1. SOUND REVIEW Use selected Sound Cards from Units 1 and 2.

2. ACCURACY AND FLUENCY BUILDING For each column, have students say any underlined part, then read each word. Next, have students read the whole column.

A1 New Sound Practice	B1 Bossy E	C1 Rhyming Words	D1 Possessives	E1 Tricky Words
saw	here	book	Albert's	been
paw	home	look	Ana's	Martinez
draw	made	nook	dad's	neighborhoods
drawing	make	**C2** Reading by Analogy	kids'	brothers
A2 Mixed Practice	**B2** Mixed Review	so	bird's	**E2** Story Words
sky	bath	no	**D2** Rhyming Words	places
fort	hang	Lopez	most	boys
girls	making	call	post	sentences
bunk	spend	also	or	
		always	door	
			floor	

3. COMPOUND WORDS Have students read each word part, then read each whole word.

A	for•ever	forever	some•where	somewhere
B	up•stairs	upstairs	bed•room	bedroom
C	where•ever	wherever	aw~~e~~•some	awesome

4. MULTISYLLABIC WORDS Have students read and finger count each word part, then read each whole word.

A	pre•tend	pretend	a•part•ment	apartment
B	kitch•en	kitchen	build•ing	building
C	to•geth•er	together	com•pu•ter	computer

5. MORPHOGRAPHS Have students practice reading "re = again" and the related words and sentences.

A	re = again	redo = do again	My drawing can be better. I will redo it.
B		recount = count again	How many were there? We need to recount them.

 9

BUILDING MASTERY (Reminder)

For each task, have students work first on accuracy and then on fluency. Have fun!

Practice words multiple times in varied ways. Have students whisper the words, squeak the words, and read the sounds and words in a rhythm.

GENTLE CORRECTIONS

If you hear an error, write the word on the board.

Have all students identify the difficult sound and then blend the word.

Periodically, repeat practice of the difficult word.

MAIN IDEA

COMPREHENSION PROCESSES

Understand, Analyze

PREP NOTE
Use an overhead of page 10 from *Exercise Book 1*, write on a transparency placed over the page, or use a paper copy.

1 MAIN IDEA INTRODUCTION

FOCUS LESSON Skills and Strategies

Demonstrate and guide the process of figuring out and writing the main idea.
Students will not write in their books. They will respond orally and watch while you write.

- Introduce the Main Idea Focus Lesson. Say something like:

  You already know how to figure out the main idea of a picture. Understanding the main idea helps you understand what you see or read.

  Today, we're going to work on figuring out the main idea of two sentences. The main idea tells who or what the sentences are about and the most important thing that is happening.

  We're going to work on a *strategy,* or a way to figure out the main idea of sentences.

2 MAIN IDEA: More Than One Subject

Identifying—Who, Action; Using—Graphic Organizer; Classifying

- Have students read the sentences, identify who the sentences are about, and then identify one word to use for the subject.

  Look at the sentences under the picture.
  Read the sentences. (Ben plays soccer. Ana plays soccer.)
  Who are the sentences about? (Ben and Ana)

  Now touch the boxes under the sentences. That diagram is called a graphic organizer.
  The graphic organizer will show how we can use one word to describe Ben and Ana.

  Let's figure out one word for Ben and Ana. (kids . . .)
  That's right. Touch the word *who.* What should I write after the word *who?* ([the kids])
  Write [the kids] on the graphic organizer.

  I can use the words [the kids] when I write my main idea.

- Have students identify the action.

  Next, we need to figure out what the important action is.
  What are Ben and Ana doing? (playing soccer . . .)
  Touch the word *Action.* What should I write under *Action?* (playing soccer)
  Write "playing soccer" on the line under "Action."

  Help me say the main idea. What should we start with? (the kids)
  Say the main idea. (The kids are playing soccer.)
  Write "The kids are playing soccer" on the line.

- Have students look at the picture. Tell them the picture illustrates the main idea of the sentences. Ask who is in the picture, what the action is, and the main idea of the picture.

  Look at the picture. The picture shows or illustrates the main idea.
  Who is the picture about? (Ben and Ana)
  What are Ben and Ana? (kids)
  Let's figure out the action. What are the kids doing? (playing soccer)
  What's the main idea of the picture? (The kids are playing soccer.)

A Bird's-Eye View

Unit 2 Exercise 2b (Focus Lesson)
Use after Exercise 2a and before Chapter 3

FOCUS LESSON
Skills and Strategies

Main Idea

Ben plays soccer. Ana plays soccer.

Ben	**Who?** the kids
Ana	

Action: What are Ben and Ana doing?

playing soccer

Main Idea:

The kids are playing soccer.

10 Blackline Master

CHAPTER 2 INSTRUCTIONS

Students read with the teacher.

COMPREHENSION PROCESSES

Understand, Apply

PROCEDURES

1. Reviewing Chapter 1

Defining and Using Vocabulary—globe, continent; Identifying—Fact

Review some of the facts learned in Chapter 1. Say something like:

Let's talk about what you learned in Chapter 1.
If we can't remember, what can we do? (look in our books)
What is a globe?
(A globe is a round map shaped like the Earth.)
What is a continent? (A continent is a vast area of land.)
What continent do we live on? ([We live on North America.])

2. Introducing Chapter 2

Identifying—Title; Defining and Using Vocabulary—neighborhood; Inferring

Discuss the chapter title. Say something like:

What's the title of this chapter of "A Bird's-Eye View"?
(Our Neighborhoods, Our Homes)
What is a neighborhood? (It's a place near us. It's where we live . . .)
Let's go back to page 33 and read the book's definition of *neighborhood.*
Everyone, read the definition. (A neighborhood is a part of a town. It is made up of people who live near each other.)
You were right. Our neighborhood is the part of town we live in.
Our neighborhood is made up of the people who . . . live near us.

3. First Reading

- Ask questions and discuss the story as indicated by the gray text.
- Mix group and individual turns, independent of your voice.
  Have students work toward a group accuracy goal of 0–4 errors.
- After reading the story, practice any difficult words. Reread the story if students have not reached the accuracy goal.

4. Second Reading, Timed Readings: Repeated Reading

- As time allows, have students do Timed Readings while others follow along.
- Time individuals for 30 seconds and encourage each child to work for a personal best.
- Determine words correct per minute. Record student scores.

5. Whisper Reading: Repeated Reading

Have students finger track and whisper read before beginning independent work.

6. Homework 2: Repeated Reading

Our Neighborhoods, Our Homes

Ana, Ben, and Maya's Neighborhood

We can make maps of our world, our continents, and our countries. We can also make maps of smaller places, like our neighborhoods. A map is like what a bird would see if it looked down from the sky. This is a bird's-eye view of the kids' neighborhood.

What does this map show?[1] Why is it called a *bird's-eye view*?[2]

COMPREHENDING AS YOU GO

❶ **Understand:** Explaining; Using Vocabulary—neighborhood (This map shows the neighborhood where Maya, Ben, and Ana live.)

❷ **Understand:** Defining and Using Idioms and Expressions—bird's-eye view (It looks like what a bird would see if it looked down from the sky.)

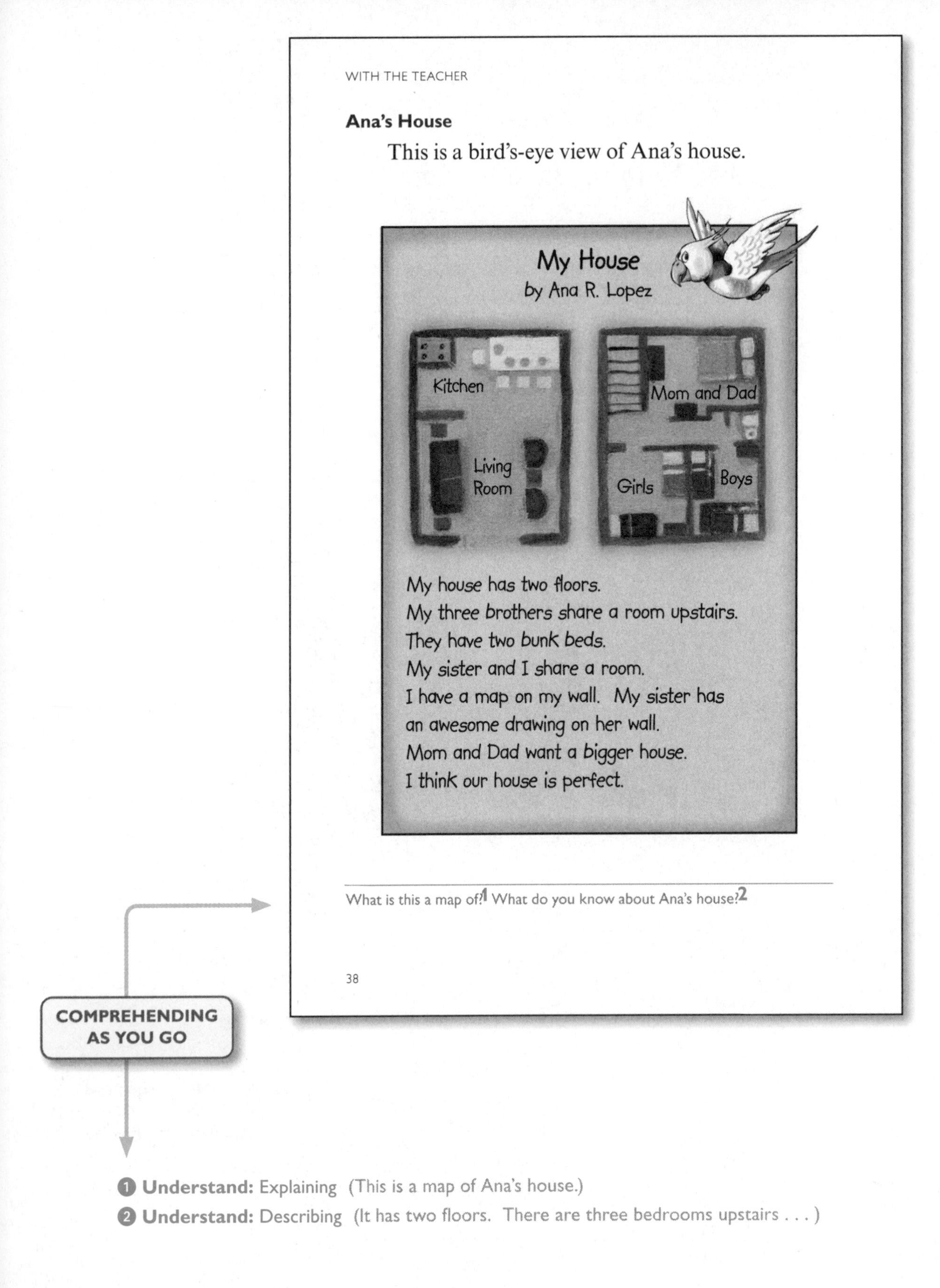

WITH THE TEACHER

Ana's House

This is a bird's-eye view of Ana's house.

My house has two floors.
My three brothers share a room upstairs.
They have two bunk beds.
My sister and I share a room.
I have a map on my wall. My sister has an awesome drawing on her wall.
Mom and Dad want a bigger house.
I think our house is perfect.

What is this a map of?[1] What do you know about Ana's house?[2]

38

COMPREHENDING AS YOU GO

1 **Understand:** Explaining (This is a map of Ana's house.)

2 **Understand:** Describing (It has two floors. There are three bedrooms upstairs . . .)

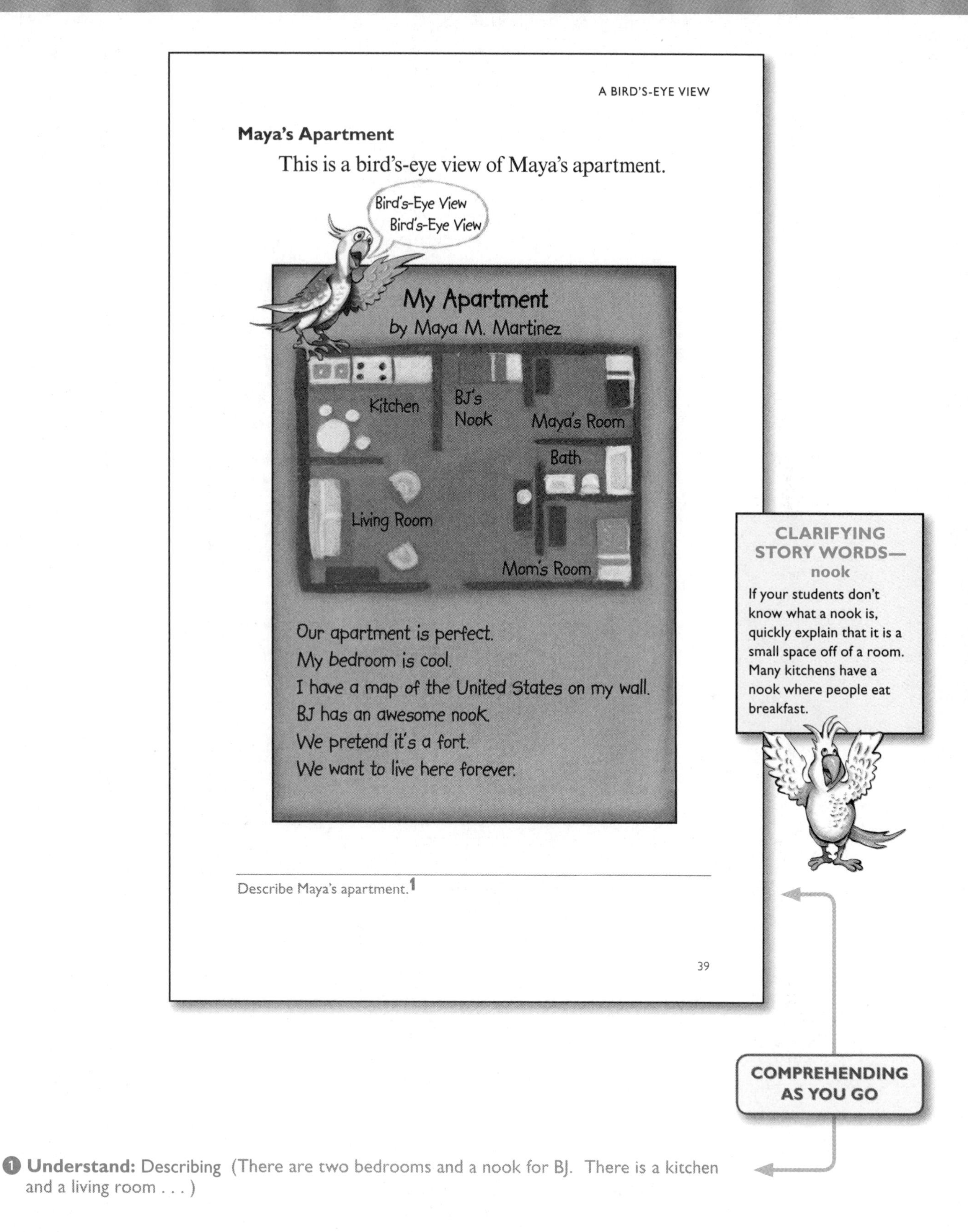

Maya's Apartment

This is a bird's-eye view of Maya's apartment.

Describe Maya's apartment.[1]

CLARIFYING STORY WORDS—nook

If your students don't know what a nook is, quickly explain that it is a small space off of a room. Many kitchens have a nook where people eat breakfast.

COMPREHENDING AS YOU GO

❶ **Understand:** Describing (There are two bedrooms and a nook for BJ. There is a kitchen and a living room . . .)

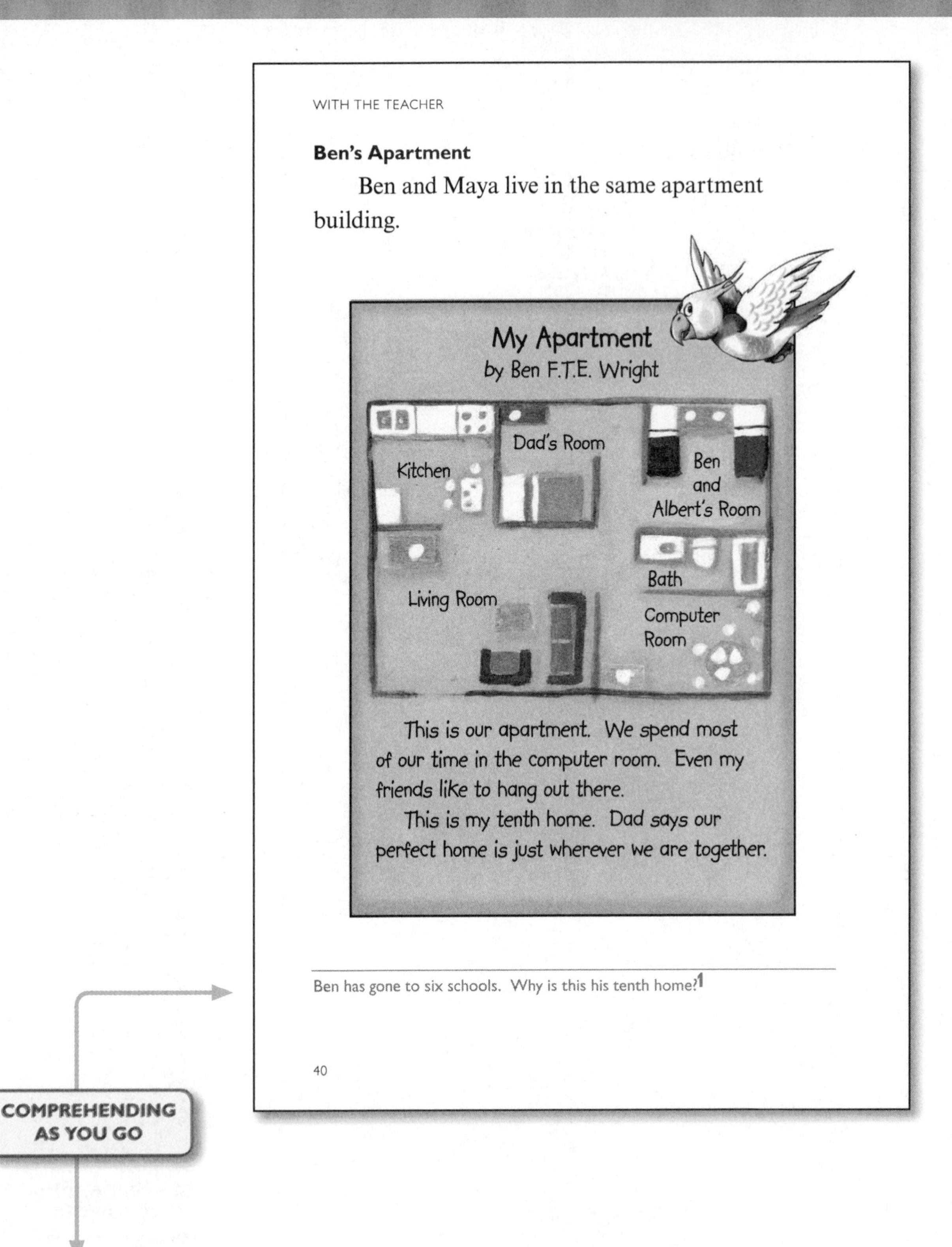

WITH THE TEACHER

Ben's Apartment

Ben and Maya live in the same apartment building.

My Apartment
by Ben F.T.E. Wright

This is our apartment. We spend most of our time in the computer room. Even my friends like to hang out there.

This is my tenth home. Dad says our perfect home is just wherever we are together.

Ben has gone to six schools. Why is this his tenth home?[1]

40

COMPREHENDING AS YOU GO

❶ **Apply:** Inferring; Explaining (Ben's family has moved a lot . . . Maybe he moved before he was old enough to go to school. Maybe he moved to a new home but went to the same school.)

Our Maps

Hi, it's me, Mr. Chapman. Look at the maps my class made. Each map is perfect! Are we good or what?

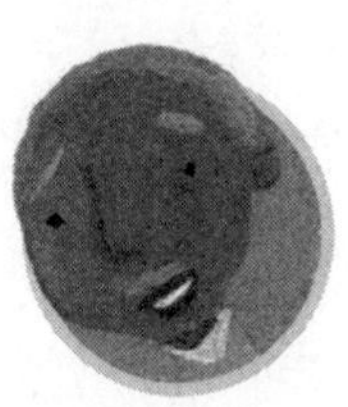

How can you tell Mr. Chapman is proud of his class?[1] How do you think the kids feel about their work?[2]

COMPREHENDING AS YOU GO

1. **Apply:** Inferring; Using Vocabulary—perfect (Mr. Chapman says their maps are perfect. This tells that Mr. Chapman is proud of his class. He looks proud. His class has done a good job . . .)
2. **Apply:** Inferring (The kids are happy with their maps. The kids are proud of their work . . .)

★PASSAGE COMPREHENSION

COMPREHENSION PROCESSES

Remember, Understand, Apply

WRITING TRAITS

Conventions—Period

Identifying—Topic

Identifying—What

Using Graphic Organizer; Identifying; Using Idioms and Expressions—bird's-eye view; Visualizing; Illustrating

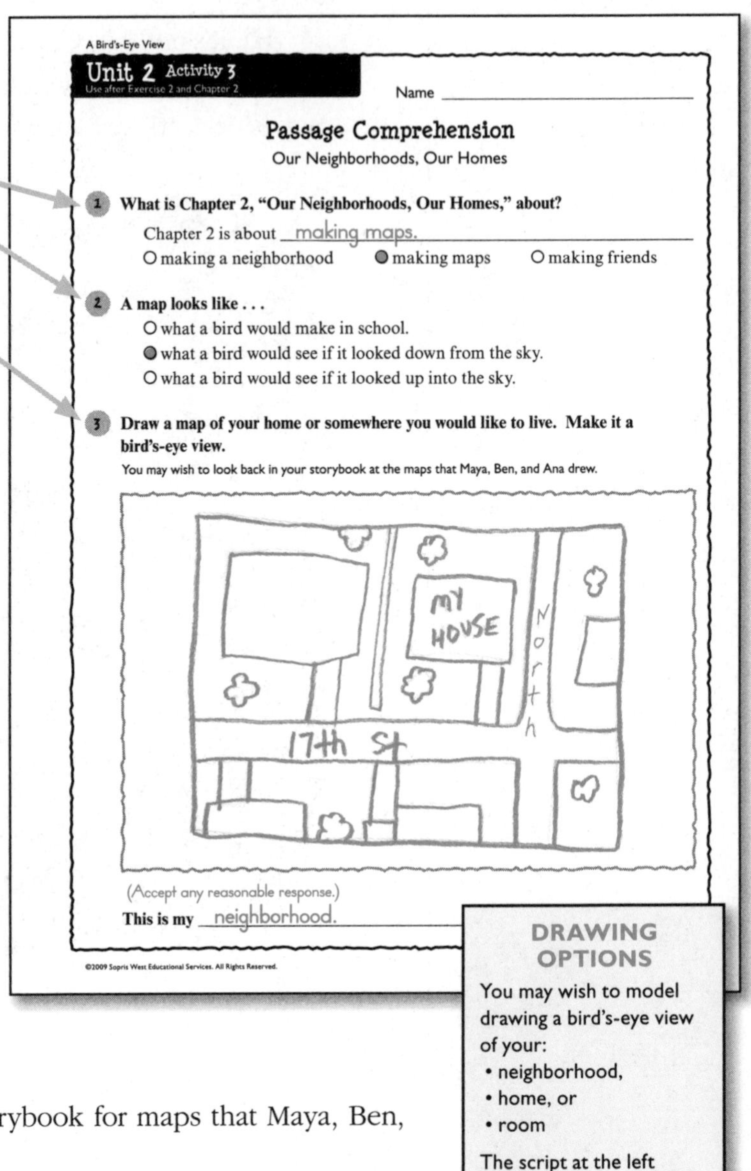

A Bird's-Eye View

Unit 2 Activity 3
Use after Exercise 2 and Chapter 2

Name ____________________

Passage Comprehension
Our Neighborhoods, Our Homes

1. **What is Chapter 2, "Our Neighborhoods, Our Homes," about?**
   Chapter 2 is about making maps.
   ○ making a neighborhood ● making maps ○ making friends

2. **A map looks like . . .**
   ○ what a bird would make in school.
   ● what a bird would see if it looked down from the sky.
   ○ what a bird would see if it looked up into the sky.

3. **Draw a map of your home or somewhere you would like to live. Make it a bird's-eye view.**
   You may wish to look back in your storybook at the maps that Maya, Ben, and Ana drew.

(Accept any reasonable response.)

This is my neighborhood.

PROCEDURES

For each step, demonstrate and guide practice, as needed. Then have students complete the page independently.

1. **Selection Response—Basic Instructions** (Items 1, 2)
   - Have students read each question or sentence, then fill in the bubble and/or blank with the correct answer.
   - Remind students to reread their sentences to make sure they are complete sentences and to put a period at the end.

2. **Map: Illustrating ★ Labeling—Specific Instructions** (Item 3)
   - Have students read the instructions and draw a map.
     Remind students to look in their storybook for maps that Maya, Ben, and Ana drew. Say something like:
     First, you need to decide what you are going to draw a map of.
     My house has an upstairs and a downstairs, but that would be too hard to draw. So I think I'll draw a bird's-eye view of the main floor in my house.

     Next, I'm going to draw an outline of the house. It's a rectangle. **Draw a rectangle.**
     Let's see. My main floor has the living room, dining room, and kitchen. There's also a bathroom and my bedroom. I think I'll start by drawing the front door so I can think about where the other rooms are. **Draw a front door.** The living room is first . . .
   - Have students read the sentence stem under the map and tell students how you would label your map. Discuss how they might complete the sentence. Remind them to put a period at the end of the sentence.

DRAWING OPTIONS

You may wish to model drawing a bird's-eye view of your:
- neighborhood,
- home, or
- room

The script at the left illustrates how to model drawing a bird's-eye view of your home.

Self-monitoring

Have students check and correct their work.

★= New in this unit

★MAIN IDEA

COMPREHENSION PROCESSES

Remember, Understand, Apply, Analyze

WRITING TRAITS

Conventions—Complete Sentence, Capital, Period

Identifying—Who

Classifying

Inferring—Main Idea

Visualizing, Illustrating

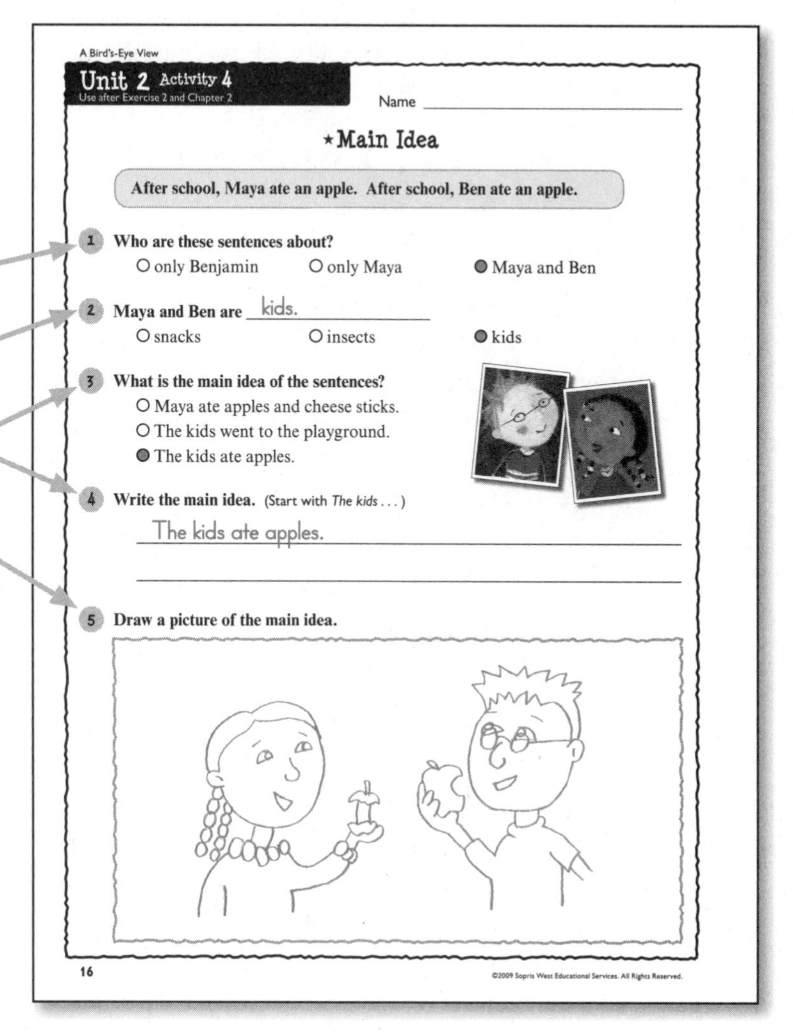
A Bird's-Eye View

Unit 2 Activity 4
Use after Exercise 2 and Chapter 2

Name

★Main Idea

After school, Maya ate an apple. After school, Ben ate an apple.

1. Who are these sentences about?
○ only Benjamin ○ only Maya ● Maya and Ben

2. Maya and Ben are kids.
○ snacks ○ insects ● kids

3. What is the main idea of the sentences?
○ Maya ate apples and cheese sticks.
○ The kids went to the playground.
● The kids ate apples.

4. Write the main idea. (Start with *The kids* . . .)
The kids ate apples.

5. Draw a picture of the main idea.

16

©2009 Sopris West Educational Services. All Rights Reserved.

PROCEDURES

For each step, demonstrate and guide practice, as needed. Then have students complete the page independently.

1. Main Idea: Selection Response—Specific Instructions (Items 1–3)

Have students read the sentences in the gray box, then fill in the bubble and/or blank with the correct answer. Remind students to put a period at the end of the sentence.

You're going to figure out the main idea, just like you did in the Focus Lesson. The main idea tells who or what the sentences are about and the most important thing that is happening. Read the sentences in the gray box. (After school, Maya ate an apple. After school, Ben ate an apple.) Read item 1. (Who are these sentences about?) What's the answer? (Maya and Ben)

Read item 2. Say "blank" when you get to the blank. (Maya and Ben are blank.) We're going to figure out what Maya and Ben are. Read the sentence with the first choice. (Maya and Ben are snacks.)

Are Maya and Ben snacks? (no) So does that answer make sense? (no)

Repeat with the second choice and third choice.

Read item 3. (What is the main idea of the sentences?) Read the first choice. (Maya ate apples and cheese sticks.) Is that what the sentences told us? (no)

Repeat with the second choice and third choice.

2. Main Idea: Sentence Writing, Illustrating—Basic Instructions (Items 4, 5)

Have students write the main idea sentence. Give them the starting phrase and remind them to use a capital and a period. Then have students illustrate the main idea.

★= New in this unit

> **PACING**
> Exercises 3a and 3b should take about 20 minutes.

❶ SOUND REVIEW

Use selected Sound Cards from Units 1 and 2.

❷ SHIFTY WORD BLENDING

For each word, have students say the underlined sound. Then have them sound out the word smoothly and say it. Use the words in sentences, as needed.

❸ ACCURACY AND FLUENCY BUILDING

> **ACCURACY AND FLUENCY BUILDING (Reminder)**
> - For each task, have students say any underlined part, then read the word.
> - Set a pace. Then have students read the whole words in each task and column.
> - Provide repeated practice, building accuracy first, then fluency.

C1. Buildups

- Tell students they can figure out bigger words by building from smaller words.
  Have students read each word. Say something like:
  You can read big words by building on smaller words.
  Read the first word. (be) Read the next, bigger word. (belong)
  Read the next, bigger word. (belonging) Read the biggest word. (belongings)
- Repeat for the next set.

C2. Related Words

Tell students the words in C2 are related to the word "move." Have students read each word.

D1. Word Endings

Have students read any underlined word, then the word with an ending.
Note: Tell students that you change the y to i-e when you add s to "family."

E1. Tricky Words

- For each Tricky Word, have students identify known sounds or word parts. Use the word in a sentence to help with pronunciation.
- If the word is unfamiliar, tell students the word. Then have students say, spell, and say it.

clothes

Try to sound out the first Tricky Word in your head.
Thumbs up when you know the word. Use my sentence to help you pronounce the word.
In the closet, we hang our . . . *clothes.* Spell *clothes.* (c-l-o-t-h-e-s)
Read the word two times. (clothes, clothes)

tables

Look at the next word. Say the word by parts with me. ta-bles
Our classroom got new chairs and . . . *tables.* Spell *tables.* (t-a-b-l-e-s) Read the word two times. (tables, tables)

❹ WORDS IN CONTEXT

- Tell students that the underlined words are tricky, but they can use the sounds and word parts they know and then the sentence to figure out how to say each word.
- Have students read each word part, the whole word, and then the sentence.

❺ MORPHOGRAPHS AND AFFIXES

- For Row A, have students read *-tion.* Next, have students read the underlined part, then the word.

- For Row B, have students read the underlined morphograph and the word, then rephrase each word. Say something like:

  Put your finger under the first word in Row B. Read the underlined part, then the word. (re, redo) What's another way to say redo? (do again)
- Repeat, as needed.

People on the Move

Unit 2 Exercise 3a
Use before Exercise 3b (Focus Lesson)

1. SOUND REVIEW Use selected Sound Cards from Units 1 and 2.

2. SHIFTY WORD BLENDING For each word, have students say the underlined part, sound out smoothly, then read the word.

them	than	plan	plane

3. ACCURACY AND FLUENCY BUILDING For each column, have students say any underlined part, then read each word. Next, have students read the whole column.

A1 New Sound Practice	B1 Bossy E	C1 Buildups	D1 Word Endings	E1 Tricky Words
law	skates	be	packed	clothes
claw	takes	belong	packing	tables
dawn	piles	belonging	couches	been
awesome	bikes	belongings	dishes	carry
A2 Mixed Practice	rode	oodles	boxes	neighborhood
tight	plane	caboodles	offered	**E2** Story Words
stacks	these	**C2** Related Words	hundreds	new
wrap		move	family	place
stuff		moved	families	sentences
squeeze		moving		
choose				

4. WORDS IN CONTEXT Have students use the sounds and word parts they know and then the sentence to pronounce each underlined word.

A	pic•ture	I will draw a picture of my cat.
B	doz•ens	There are dozens of countries on the map.
C	suit•cases	We packed the suitcases in the car.
D	ad•ven•ture	Miss Tam went on an adventure to a dino dig.

5. MORPHOGRAPHS AND AFFIXES Have students read the underlined word part, then the word.

A	-tion	action	fiction	attention
B	re-	redo	recount	replay

11

LEARNING FROM MISTAKES (Reminder)

Mistakes are an important part of learning!

- If you hear a mistake, say something like:

  Oops, that was hard, but we can get it!
- Demonstrate or guide students on the correct skill or strategy (sound, sounding out, reading a word by parts . . .).
- Have the group practice the skill.
- Make sure the individual who made the mistake has an opportunity to demonstrate that he or she worked hard and got it.

Give descriptive feedback:

[Kristin], you worked hard and now you can read the Tricky Word *neighborhood*.

CHARACTERIZATION

> **PREP NOTE**
> Use an overhead of page 12 from *Exercise Book 1*, write on a transparency placed over the page, or use a paper copy.

COMPREHENSION PROCESSES

Remember, Understand, Analyze

1 CHARACTERIZATION INTRODUCTION

Demonstrate and guide the process of completing a character web. Students will not write in their books. They will respond orally and watch while you write.

FOCUS LESSON Skills and Strategies

Introduce the Characterization Focus Lesson. Say something like:

Today, we're going to fill out a character web. A character web will help us remember important things about a character.

2 USING A CHARACTER WEB

Using—Graphic Organizer; Identifying—Main Character; Drawing Conclusions

- Demonstrate and guide how to complete the character web.

  Look at page 12. This shows a character web.

  Who is this character web about? (Ben)

  That's right—it's about Ben. Let's think about what we know about Ben.

  We know that he likes computers, so we can write "likes computers" on the web.

  Write "likes computers" on the web.

  What else do we know about Ben? (He moves around a lot, has a friend named Maya, is in second grade, has a brother named Albert . . .)

  Write "moves around, friend Maya, second grade" on the web.

  What are words that describe Ben? (likes computers . . .)

- Demonstrate how to draw conclusions about the character by using the web.

  Now that we have a character web, we can tell more about Ben. This is what I might say if someone asked me what Ben was like. I might say, "Ben is an interesting second grader. He has moved around a lot, so he knows about many places around the world. He knows a lot about computers because his dad is a computer scientist. In the Bronx, Ben has made a good friend named Maya."

- Tell students that they can always add more words to a character web as they read and learn more about the character. Explain that getting to know a story character is like getting to know someone. You keep learning more.

  Note: The character web will become an important part of story mapping.

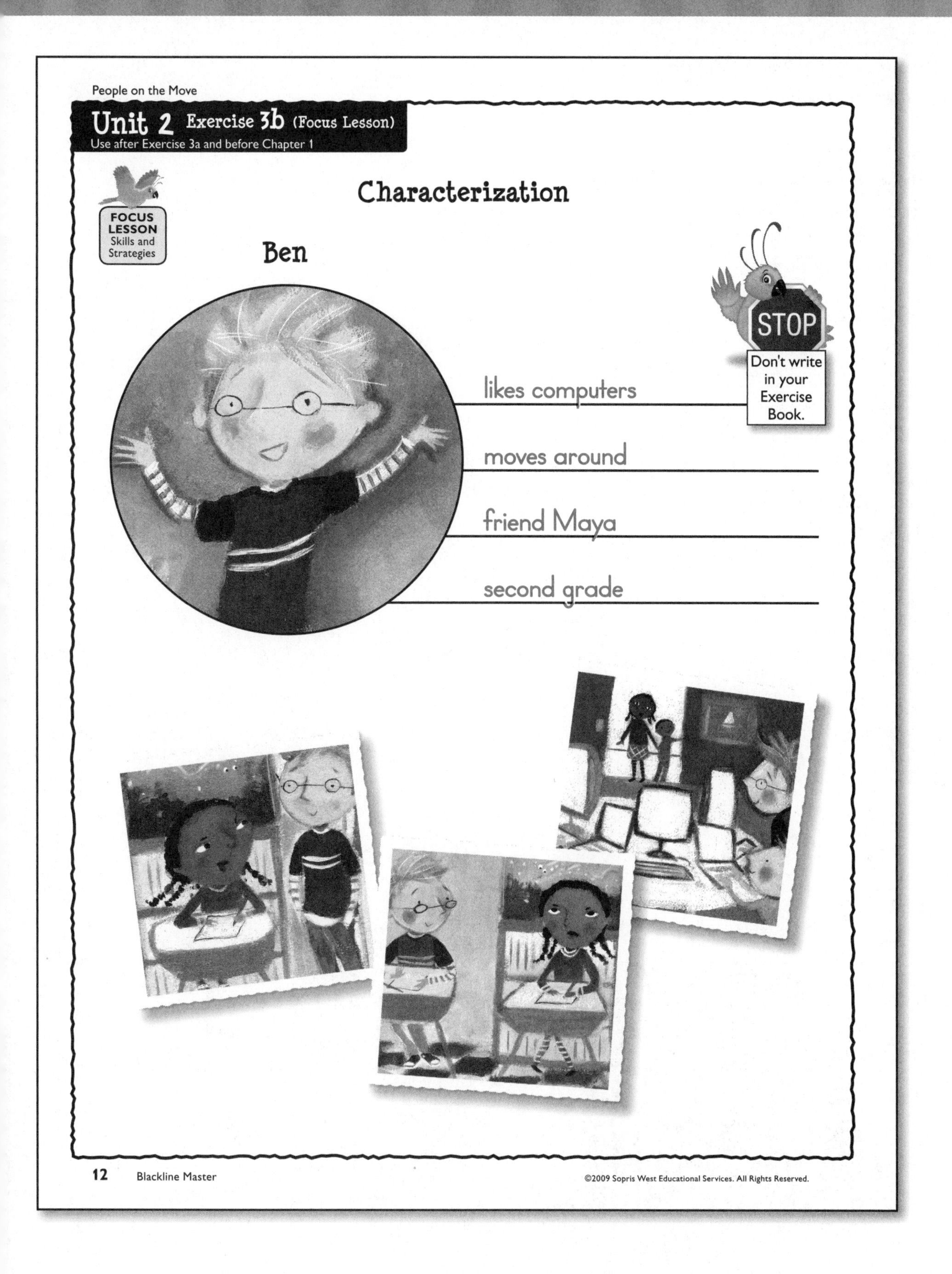

People on the Move
Unit 2 Exercise 3b (Focus Lesson)
Use after Exercise 3a and before Chapter 1
FOCUS LESSON
Skills and Strategies
Characterization
Ben
STOP
Don't write in your Exercise Book.
likes computers
moves around
friend Maya
second grade
12 Blackline Master
©2009 Sopris West Educational Services. All Rights Reserved.

COMPREHENSION PROCESSES

Understand, Apply

PROCEDURES

Introducing the Story and Title Page

Identifying—Title, Illustrator; Inferring; Making Connections

- Have students turn to storybook page 42. Say something like:

  Look at the title page.
  What is our next story called? (People on the Move)
  There are many authors of this story. Jessica Sprick, Marilyn Sprick, Ann Watanabe, and Karen Akiyama-Paik all worked together to write this story.
  Who is the illustrator? (Jana Christy)

  Look at the picture and think about the title.
  What do you think this story is about?
  (traveling, moving, going new places, a long trip . . .)

  Raise your hand if you've ever moved. You will have fun with this story.

- Discuss the gray text questions under the picture.

Look at the family. What are they doing?[1] Where do you think they are going?[2]

42

1. **Understand:** Describing (They are sitting down. They are on a boat . . .)
2. **Apply:** Predicting (They are going on a trip. They are moving . . .)

MODEL ENTHUSIASM (Reminder)

To encourage students' interest in the topic, think aloud. Model your enthusiasm. Say something like:

I think "People on the Move" is going to be an interesting story. How many of you have moved? [Five] of us have moved. What was it like to move?

COMPREHENSION PROCESSES

Understand, Apply

PROCEDURES

Introducing Vocabulary

★ **immigrant** ★ **relative**
★ **cram** ★ **belongings**
★ **tradition**

- For each vocabulary word, have students read the word by parts, then read the whole word.
- Read the student-friendly explanations to students as they follow with their fingers. Then have students use the vocabulary word by following the gray text.
- Review and discuss the illustrations, as appropriate.

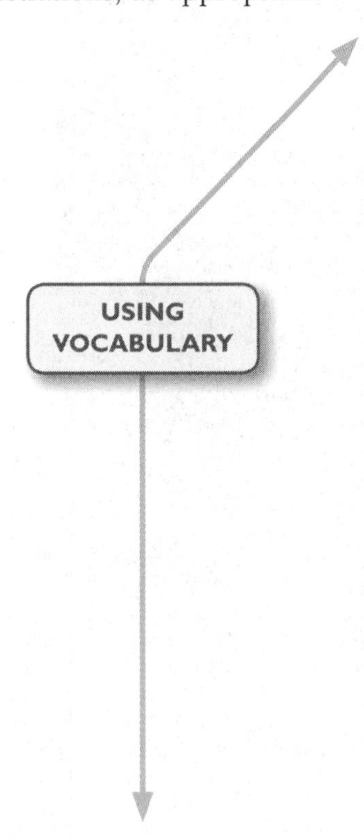

WITH THE TEACHER

Chapters 1–3

Vocabulary

★ **im•mi•grant**

A person who moves from one country to another is called an **immigrant**.

People who move from England to the United States are . . .[1] People who move from the United States to Canada are . . .[2]

★ **re•la•tive**

A **relative** is a person who is part of your family. Relatives are people who were born, adopted, or married into your family.

Our *relatives* all came to my sister's wedding. My cousins, aunts, and uncles came from far away to join us. Name some of your relatives.[3]

★ **cram**

Cram means to stuff things or people into small places.

We *crammed* our clothes into the suitcase. It was so packed, we could barely close it. Look at the picture. What are the kids doing?[4]

★ = New

43

❶ **Understand:** Using Vocabulary—immigrant (immigrants)

❷ **Understand:** Using Vocabulary—immigrant (immigrants)

❸ **Apply:** Using Vocabulary—relative; Making Connections (Some of my relatives are [my grandmother, my Uncle Marty, my sister . . .])

❹ **Understand:** Describing, Using Vocabulary—cram (The kids are cramming their suitcase full of clothes.)

★ = New in this unit

WITH THE TEACHER

★ **be•long•ings**

Belongings are things that you own. They belong to you.

Sam packed his *belongings* in his backpack. He was sleeping over at Grandpa's house. What do you think Sam packed?[1]

★ **tra•di•tion**

A **tradition** is a belief or a way of doing something that families pass on to their children.

In some families, it is a *tradition* to eat turkey on Thanksgiving Day. Do you have any special traditions on Valentine's Day?[2]

44

USING VOCABULARY

❶ **Apply:** Inferring; **Understand:** Defining and Using Vocabulary—belongings (Sam packed his belongings. He probably packed his toothbrush, pajamas, pillow, baseball . . .)

❷ **Apply:** Using Vocabulary—tradition; Making Connections (One tradition is to make valentines for all my friends. My dad gets us flowers on Valentine's Day . . .)

CHAPTER 1 INSTRUCTIONS

Students read with the teacher.

COMPREHENSION PROCESSES

Remember, Understand, Apply

PROCEDURES

1. Introducing the Chapter

Identifying—Title; Inferring

Discuss the title. Say something like:
What's the title? (Oodles and Caboodles)
What do you think that means? (lots and lots of something)
What do you think oodles and caboodles have to do with moving?
(You have to move a lot of stuff.)
As you read, think about what it was like to move all your belongings.

We're going to start this chapter with a poem about moving.
Poems are made up of short lines and often have a little rhythm and/or rhyme.

2. First Reading

- Ask questions and discuss the text as indicated by the gray text. If students have difficulty comprehending, think aloud with them or reread the portion of the story that answers the question. Repeat the question.
- Mix group and individual turns, independent of your voice.
- After reading the story, practice any difficult words and reread.

> **CORRECTING DECODING ERRORS (Reminder)**
> During story reading, gently correct any error, then have students reread the sentence.

3. Second Reading, Short Passage Practice: Developing Prosody

- Demonstrate expressive, fluent reading of the verse. Say something like:
  "On the Move" isn't a story. What is it? (a poem)
  Listen to me read the first verse. This is a perky little poem, so I'm going to read it with a little snap. I'm going to give it rhythm by pausing at the commas.
  "Wrap it, stack it, stuff it in a box!
  Piles of clothes, stacks of dishes . . . "
- Guide practice with your voice.
  Read the first verse of the poem with me.
- Provide individual turns while others track with their fingers and whisper read. Provide descriptive, positive feedback.
  [Bruce], I liked the way you drew out "Oodles and caboodles of jam-packed boxes."
  Everyone, close your eyes and imagine those jam-packed boxes.
- Repeat with one paragraph or page at a time.

> **COMPREHENSION BUILDING (Reminder)**
> Encourage students to answer questions with complete sentences. If students have difficulty comprehending, think aloud with them or reread the portion of the story that answers the question. Repeat the question.

4. Whisper Reading: Repeated Reading

5. Homework 3: Repeated Reading

Oodles and Caboodles

Wrap it, stack it, stuff it in a box!
Piles of clothes, stacks of dishes,
Hundreds of pictures,
Dozens of books,
Oodles and caboodles
Of jam-packed boxes.

Pack it, stack it, squeeze it tight!
Boxes, suitcases, skates, and bikes,
Couches, beds, tables, and chairs,
Oodles and caboodles of important stuff.
It's moving day!

POEM

Genre—poetry

After reading the poem in the box, say something like:

That was fun. This part of the chapter isn't written like a story. The lines are short and it has a little rhythm. What do you call it? (a poem)

Let's read the poem again, just for fun.

Have you ever moved?[1] Where did you live?[2] What was it like to pack all your *belongings*?[3]

COMPREHENDING AS YOU GO

1. **Remember:** Identifying (yes, no . . .)
2. **Remember:** Identifying—Where (We lived in Oklahoma. We moved to a new apartment that was bigger . . .)
3. **Apply:** Making Connections; Using Vocabulary—belongings (It was a lot of work. We borrowed a big truck. We moved all our belongings . . .)

WITH THE TEACHER

People come and people go. People are always on the move. They move from one place to another—over land and sea, by train, plane, bus, and car. Sometimes even on foot.

Think about packing everything you have and moving it to a new place. Could you really take everything? How many boxes would you need? Could you send it by plane? Could you pack it in your car? Could you carry everything you have on your back?

People are moving all the time. Did you know that many families move one time every five years? That takes oodles and caboodles of boxes! Packing all your belongings is a lot of work.

How often do many families move?[1] Why do you think they move?[2]

46

VISUALIZING

Have students close their eyes and imagine putting all of their belongings in boxes and suitcases. Say something like:
Imagine all the things that belong to you being packed up. What do you see?

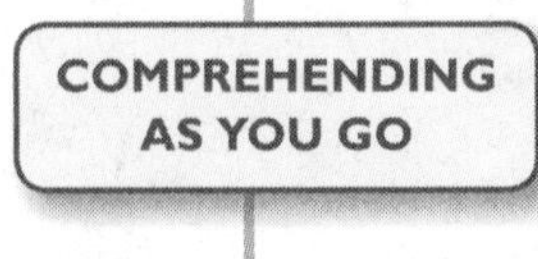

1. **Remember:** Identifying—How Often (Many families move one time every five years.)
2. **Apply:** Inferring, Making Connections (They move to a better apartment. Their mom or dad gets a new job . . .)

Why do people move?
Sometimes people have to move.
Sometimes people choose to move.

People move to start a job, to be near family, or just to have an adventure. Most people move to find a better life.

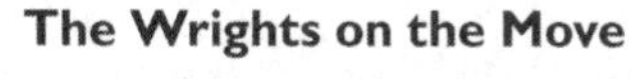

The Wrights on the Move

Name some reasons why people move.[1] Look at the picture. Why are Ben and his family moving again?[2] Do you think moving is *bittersweet* for Ben? Why or why not?[3]

LOCATING INFORMATION

After students name some reasons people move, have them locate and read the words in the text that support their responses.

[Josh] said that sometimes people move to get a bigger apartment. [Josh] came up with a great example of people moving to find a better life. Find the sentence that says, "Most people move to find a better life."

COMPREHENDING AS YOU GO

❶ **Understand:** Explaining (People move to start a job, to be near family, to have an adventure . . .)

❷ **Understand:** Explaining (Their dad has a new job offer at a dino dig.)

❸ **Apply:** Inferring; Explaining; Using Vocabulary—bittersweet (Yes, it is bittersweet. He is excited about the dino dig, but he will be sad to leave his friends.)

PASSAGE COMPREHENSION

COMPREHENSION PROCESSES

Remember, Understand, Apply, Evaluate, Create

WRITING TRAITS—BONUS

Conventions—Complete Sentence, Beginning Capital, Period

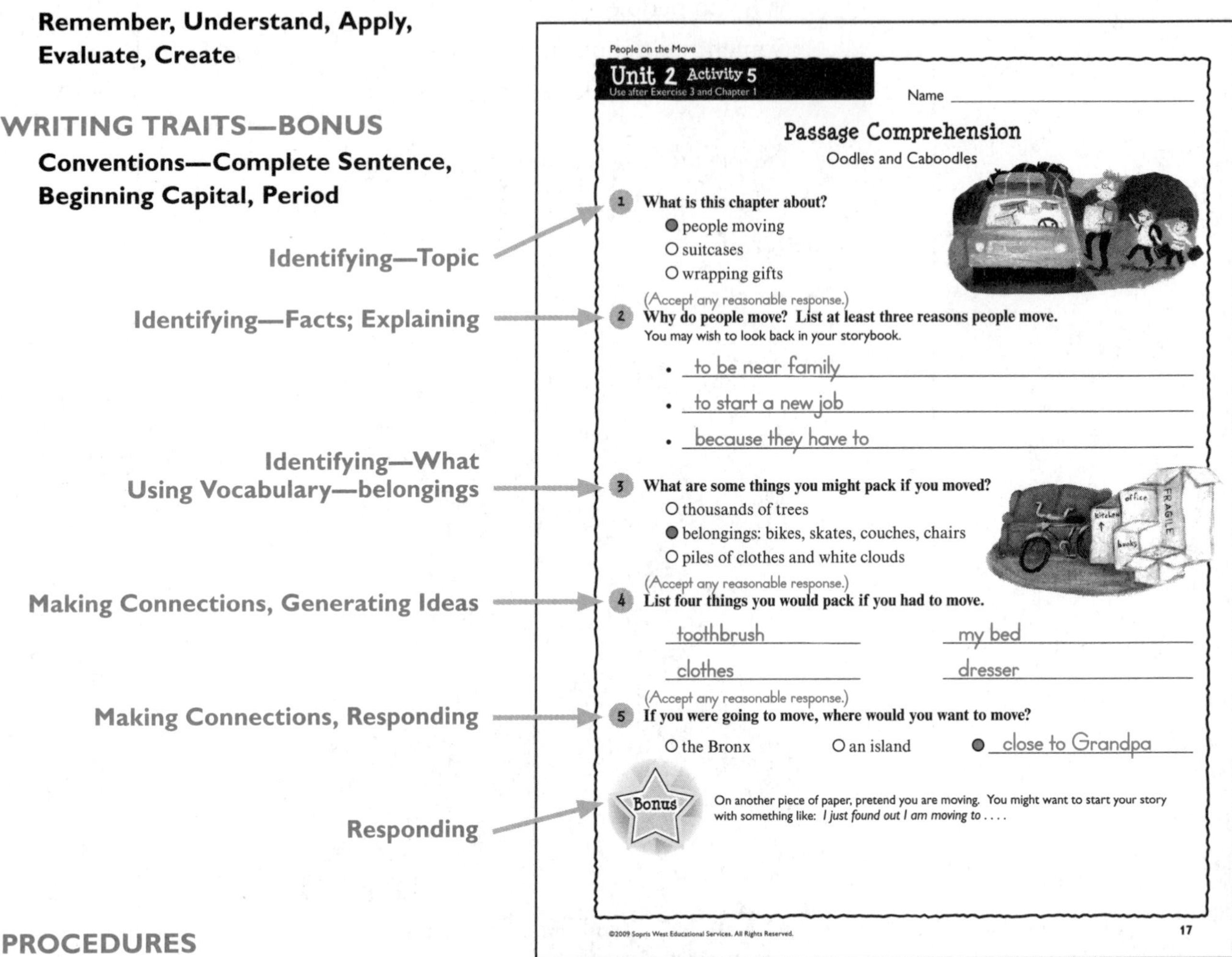

People on the Move

Unit 2 Activity 5
Use after Exercise 3 and Chapter 1

Name ____________________

Passage Comprehension

Oodles and Caboodles

1. **What is this chapter about?**
   - ● people moving
   - ○ suitcases
   - ○ wrapping gifts

(Accept any reasonable response.)

2. **Why do people move? List at least three reasons people move.**
   You may wish to look back in your storybook.
   - to be near family
   - to start a new job
   - because they have to

3. **What are some things you might pack if you moved?**
   - ○ thousands of trees
   - ● belongings: bikes, skates, couches, chairs
   - ○ piles of clothes and white clouds

(Accept any reasonable response.)

4. **List four things you would pack if you had to move.**
   toothbrush   my bed
   clothes   dresser

(Accept any reasonable response.)

5. **If you were going to move, where would you want to move?**
   ○ the Bronx   ○ an island   ● close to Grandpa

Bonus: On another piece of paper, pretend you are moving. You might want to start your story with something like: *I just found out I am moving to . . . .*

 17

PROCEDURES

For each step, demonstrate and guide practice, as needed. Then have students complete the page independently.

1. **Selection Response—Basic Instructions** (Items 1, 3, 5)
   Have students read each question or sentence, then fill in the bubble and/or blank with the correct answer.

★ 2. **Making Lists—Basic Instructions** (Items 2, 4)
   - Have students read the directions for Item 2 and brainstorm possible answers. Assist, as needed. Say something like: Who remembers why people move?
     (People move to start a job, be near family, have an adventure, find a better life . . .)
   - Have students write three reasons in the blanks.
     Note: Lists do not require complete-sentence responses.
   - Repeat procedure for Item 4.

Self-monitoring

Have students check and correct their work.

★ = New in this unit

VOCABULARY and ALPHABETICAL ORDER

COMPREHENSION PROCESSES

Remember, Understand, Apply

WRITING TRAITS

Conventions—Period

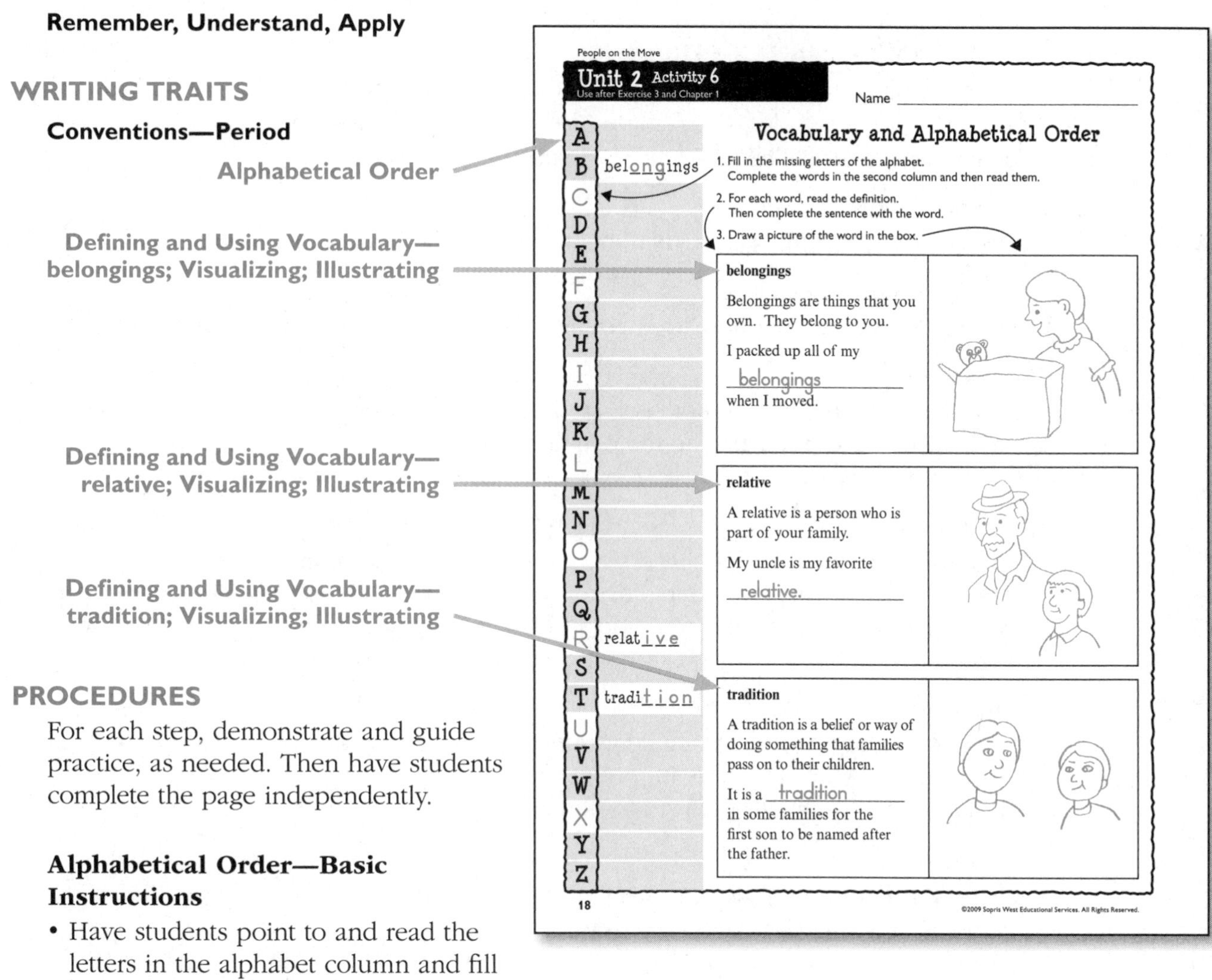

People on the Move

Unit 2 Activity 6
Use after Exercise 3 and Chapter 1

Name ____________

Vocabulary and Alphabetical Order

1. Fill in the missing letters of the alphabet. Complete the words in the second column and then read them.
2. For each word, read the definition. Then complete the sentence with the word.
3. Draw a picture of the word in the box.

A B C D E F G H I J K L M N O P Q R S T U V W X Y Z

belongings
relative
tradition

belongings
Belongings are things that you own. They belong to you.
I packed up all of my belongings when I moved.

relative
A relative is a person who is part of your family.
My uncle is my favorite relative.

tradition
A tradition is a belief or way of doing something that families pass on to their children.
It is a tradition in some families for the first son to be named after the father.

18

©2009 Sopris West Educational Services. All Rights Reserved.

PROCEDURES

For each step, demonstrate and guide practice, as needed. Then have students complete the page independently.

Alphabetical Order—Basic Instructions

- Have students point to and read the letters in the alphabet column and fill in the missing letters.
  Say the letters in alphabetical order. (A, B . . . C) Write C in the blank space.
  Say the next letters. (D, E . . . F) Write F in the blank.
  Repeat until the alphabet is complete.
- Tell students that the words in the column are in alphabetical order. Have them complete the spelling of the words by filling in the blanks.

Vocabulary: Sentence Completion—Basic Instructions

- Have students read the vocabulary words and definitions.
- Have students read the sample sentence and fill in the blank with the vocabulary word. Then have them visualize how to draw a picture to illustrate the word or sentence.
  Say something like:
  When I imagine packing up all my belongings, I imagine stacks and stacks of boxes with all my belongings lying around. That's what I'm going to draw—stacks of boxes with my things lying around. So first I'll draw the boxes . . .

Self-monitoring

Have students check and correct their work.

❶ SOUND REVIEW

Have students read the sounds and key word phrases. Work for accuracy, then fluency.

Read the sounds and the phrases. (/aw/ as in paw, /īīī/ as in flight, /ēēē/ as in eagle, /ou/ as in cloud)

❷ ACCURACY AND FLUENCY BUILDING

- For each task, have students say any underlined part, then read the word.
- Set a pace. Then have students read the whole words in each task and column.
- Provide repeated practice, building accuracy first, then fluency.

A2. Rhyming Words

Have students read the words, then identify what's the same about them.

B1. Reading by Analogy

Have students figure out how to say *o-* and *al-* by reading other words they know.

B2. Contractions

- Have students read "were not." Tell students the next word is a short way to say "were not." Then have students read the contraction.
- Repeat with "what's."

D1. Word Endings

Have students read any underlined word, then the word with an ending.

Note: Tell students that you double the m when you add *-ed* to "cram." Tell students that you change the y to i-e when you add s to "story," and you drop the e when you add y to "tasty."

E1. Tricky Words

- For each Tricky Word, have students identify known sounds or word parts. Use the word in a sentence to help with pronunciation.
- If the word is unfamiliar, tell students the word.

wonderful

Look at the first word. Say the word by parts with me. won-der-ful

Wow, what you did was amazing. It was . . . *wonderful.*

Read the word two times. (wonderful, wonderful)

languages

Look at the next word. That word is *languages*. Say the word. (languages)

I would like to learn to speak many . . . *languages.*

Read the word three times. (languages, languages, languages)

colorful I used my crayons to . . . *color.* My picture was very . . . *colorful.*

women Girls grow up to be . . . *women.*

anyone Sheila felt lonely at the new school because she didn't know . . . *anyone.*

early If you go to bed late, you won't feel like getting up . . . *early.*

earliest Juan gets up before anyone else. Juan gets up . . . *earliest.*

❸ MULTISYLLABIC WORDS

For each word, have students read each syllable, then read the whole word. Use the word in a sentence, as appropriate.

4 AFFIXES

- Have students read the affix. Next, have students read the underlined part, then the word.
- Have students go back and read whole words. Repeat practice, mixing group and individual turns.

People on the Move

Unit 2 Exercise 4

Use before Chapter 2

1. SOUND REVIEW Have students review sounds for accuracy, then for fluency.

A	aw as in paw	igh as in flight	ea as in eagle	ou as in cloud		
B	i_e	ai	ir	a_e	ch	er

2. ACCURACY AND FLUENCY BUILDING For each column, have students say any underlined part, then read each word. Next, have students read the whole column.

A1 Mixed Review	B1 Reading by Analogy	C1 Places	D1 Word Endings	E1 Tricky Words
blocks	no	Asia	crammed	wonderful
called	go	Japan	shared	languages
carts	Mexico	United States	scientists	colorful
awful	ball	Mexico	story	women
across	also	Spain	stories	anyone
strip	always	**C2 Related Words**	taste	early
these	**B2 Contractions**	im•mi•grate	tasty	earliest
least	were not	im•mi•grant	**D2 Story Words**	country
A2 Rhyming Words	weren't	im•mi•grants	boat	pull
kind	what is	im•mi•grat•ing	few	
mind	what's		spaces	
hind				
behind				

3. MULTISYLLABIC WORDS Have students read each word part, then read each whole word.

A	in•volv~~e~~s	involves	wa•gons	wagons
B	cus•toms	customs	ex•ists	exists
C	chil•dren	children	his•tor•y	history
D	dif•fer•ent	different	rel•a•tives	relatives
E	prob•a•bly	probably	grand•par•ents	grandparents

4. AFFIXES Have students read the underlined word part, then the word.

-tion	action	fiction	tra•di•tion	tradition

 13

BUILDING INDEPENDENCE (Reminder)

Some students will try to follow your voice instead of learning to read the sounds and words. Therefore, it is important for you to demonstrate and guide practice only as needed.

Give students many opportunities to respond without your assistance—with groups and individuals. Encourage independence.

CHAPTER 2 INSTRUCTIONS

Students read Chapter 2 with the teacher.

COMPREHENSION PROCESSES

Understand, Apply, Create

PROCEDURES

1. Introducing Chapter 2

Identifying—Title; Inferring

Discuss the title. Say something like:

We're reading a story called "People on the Move."

What's the name of this chapter? (From Here to There)

What do you think this passage is about? (people who move from here to there, from one place to another by car, boat, plane . . .)

2. First Reading

- Ask questions and discuss the story as indicated by the gray text.
- Mix group and individual turns, independent of your voice.
  Have students work toward a group accuracy goal of 0–5 errors.
  Quietly keep track of errors made by all students in the group.
- After reading the story, practice any difficult words.
  Reread the story if students have not reached the accuracy goal.

3. Second Reading, Timed Readings: Repeated Reading

- As time allows, have students do Timed Readings while others follow along.
- Time individuals for 30 seconds and encourage each child to work for a personal best.
- Count the number of words read correctly in 30 seconds (words read minus errors). Multiply by two to determine words correct per minute. Record student scores.

4. Whisper Reading: Repeated Reading

Have students finger track and whisper read before beginning independent work.

5. Homework 4: Repeated Reading

From Here to There

If you live in the United States, you've probably moved at least one time. You may have moved a few blocks, all the way across town, or to a different state. You may have traveled by car, bus, train, plane, or even in a ship.

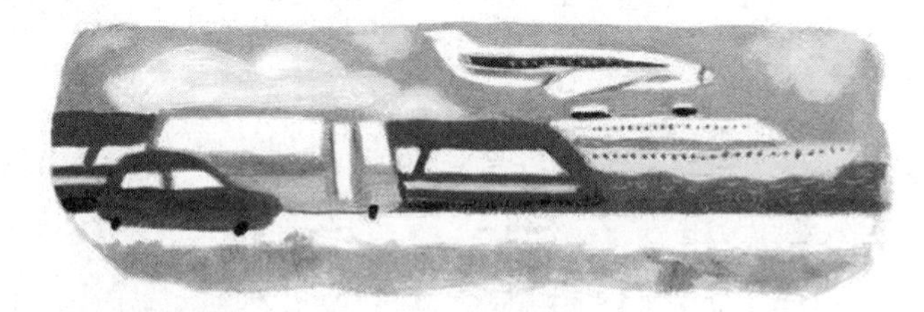

From Country to Country

Some people move from one country to another. These people are called immigrants. You, your parents, your grandparents, your great-grandparents, or even your great-great-grandparents may have come to America from another country.

When people move from country to country, what are they called? 1

48

MAKING CONNECTIONS

Using Vocabulary—immigrant

After completing the page, say something like:

Read the last sentence again. (You, your parents, your grandparents, your great-grandparents, or even your great-great-grandparents may have come to America from another country.) Raise your hand if someone in your family is an immigrant.

[Andrew], who in your family moved to this country?

COMPREHENDING AS YOU GO

1 **Understand:** Defining and Using Vocabulary—immigrant (Someone who moves from one country to another is called an immigrant.)

PEOPLE ON THE MOVE

The Earliest Americans

Thousands of years ago, there weren't any people in America. Some scientists think that the first people came to our continent about 14,000 years ago. They came looking for food. These people may have walked from Asia to America on a strip of land that no longer exists.

Think about walking and carrying all your belongings for months at a time!

How do some scientists think the first *immigrants* came to America?[1] What do you think this trip would have been like?[2]

49

BUILDING COMPREHENSION (Reminder)

Encourage students to answer questions with complete sentences. If students answer a question with a one-word response, help them elaborate and/or construct a complete answer. Say something like:

What do you think the trip would have been like? (hard)

I'm sure it was hard. Tell me why. Start your sentence with "It was hard because . . . " (It was hard because people had to walk and carry all their belongings.)

That's great. You used a complete sentence, and you told me more details.

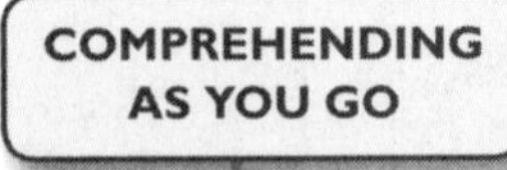

1. **Understand:** Explaining; Using Vocabulary—immigrant (Scientists think the first immigrants walked from Asia to America.)
2. **Apply:** Inferring; Explaining; Using Vocabulary—belongings (It would have been hard to walk so far. The people in the picture look cold and tired. It would have been hard to carry all your belongings . . .)

WITH THE TEACHER

Immigrants 200 Years Ago

Before there were planes and cars, immigrating to any country was very hard. People walked. They rode on animals. They rode in carts and covered wagons pulled by animals.

Many immigrants traveled by boat. Men, women, and children were often crammed into small spaces for weeks at a time. Many immigrants had to leave most of their belongings behind.

Imagine moving all your belongings in a crowded boat.

Describe what you think it would have been like to travel for weeks on a crowded boat.[1] What would you have done to pass the time?[2]

50

COMPREHENDING AS YOU GO

1. **Apply:** Inferring; **Understand:** Describing (It would have been very boring. There wouldn't have been anything to do . . .)
2. **Create:** Making Connections, Generating Ideas (I would have read a book, talked to others, kept a journal, drawn pictures . . .)

Immigrants Today

Today, people are still moving to America. People come by boat, but they also travel by car, bus, train, and plane. Has anyone in your class moved from another country? Is anyone from Spain, Mexico, Japan, or Ghana? Where are you or your relatives from?

Today some people immigrate to another country by plane.

Name some ways people immigrate today.[1] Which way would you choose to travel? Why?[2]

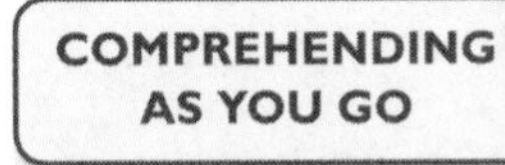

❶ **Remember:** Identifying; **Apply:** Using Vocabulary—immigrate (People immigrate by boat, car, bus, train, and plane.)

❷ **Evaluate:** Responding; **Apply:** Explaining (I would travel by car so that I could see everything on the way to our new home.)

Over hundreds of years, immigrants have shared their colorful customs, tasty foods, and the rich sounds of many languages.

America is a wonderful mix of people and traditions from places all around the world.

More than 300 languages are spoken in the United States.

Family Stories

Everyone has a story to tell about his or her family's history. The story may involve a move, even if it was way back in time.

What is your family's history?[1]

MAKING CONNECTIONS

As time allows, you may wish to make a list of the countries your students' relatives are from or identify these countries on a map.

COMPREHENDING AS YOU GO

1 **Apply:** Making Connections, Explaining (My grandma lives in Mexico. I was born in Utah . . .)

PASSAGE COMPREHENSION

COMPREHENSION PROCESSES

Remember, Understand, Apply

WRITING TRAITS

Conventions—Period

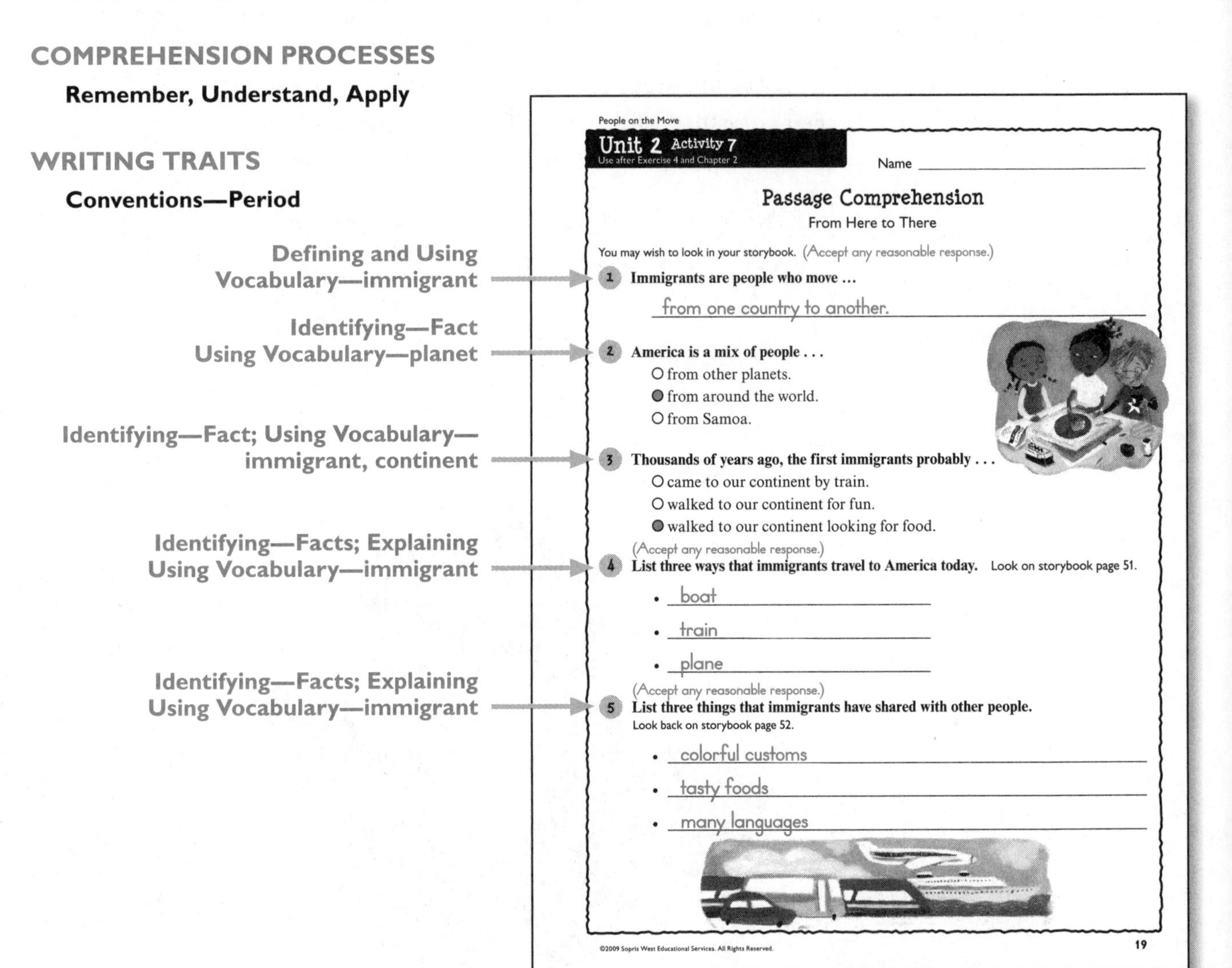

Defining and Using Vocabulary—immigrant

Identifying—Fact
Using Vocabulary—planet

Identifying—Fact; Using Vocabulary—immigrant, continent

Identifying—Facts; Explaining
Using Vocabulary—immigrant

Identifying—Facts; Explaining
Using Vocabulary—immigrant

People on the Move

Unit 2 Activity 7
Use after Exercise 4 and Chapter 2

Name ______________

Passage Comprehension

From Here to There

You may wish to look in your storybook. (Accept any reasonable response.)

1. **Immigrants are people who move ...**
   from one country to another.

2. **America is a mix of people . . .**
   - ○ from other planets.
   - ● from around the world.
   - ○ from Samoa.

3. **Thousands of years ago, the first immigrants probably . . .**
   - ○ came to our continent by train.
   - ○ walked to our continent for fun.
   - ● walked to our continent looking for food.

(Accept any reasonable response.)

4. **List three ways that immigrants travel to America today.** Look on storybook page 51.
   - boat
   - train
   - plane

(Accept any reasonable response.)

5. **List three things that immigrants have shared with other people.**
   Look back on storybook page 52.
   - colorful customs
   - tasty foods
   - many languages

©2009 Sopris West Educational Services. All Rights Reserved.

19

PROCEDURES

For each step, demonstrate and guide practice, as needed. Then have students complete the page independently.

1. **Selection Response—Basic Instructions** (Items 1–3)
   Have students read each question or sentence, then fill in the bubble and/or blank with the correct answer. Remind students to put a period at the end of the sentence.

2. **Making Lists—Basic Instructions** (Items 4, 5)
   - Have students read the directions and brainstorm possible answers. Have students read the small print to find where to look back in the storybook, if needed.
   - Have students write the answers in the blanks.

Self-monitoring

Have students check and correct their work.

MAIN IDEA

COMPREHENSION PROCESSES

Remember, Understand, Apply, Analyze

WRITING TRAITS

Conventions—Complete Sentence, Capital, Period

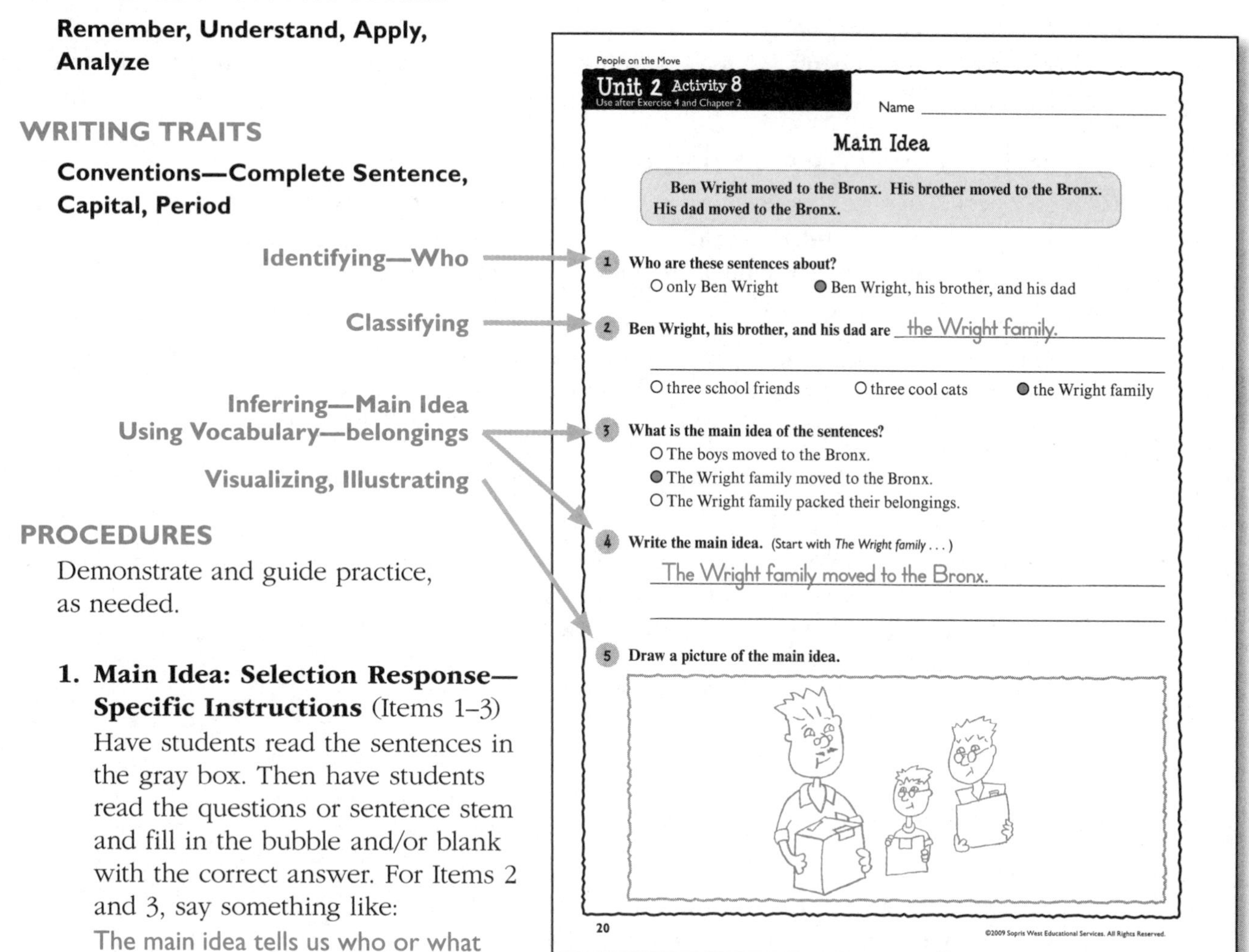

People on the Move

Unit 2 Activity 8
Use after Exercise 4 and Chapter 2

Name ______________________

Main Idea

> Ben Wright moved to the Bronx. His brother moved to the Bronx. His dad moved to the Bronx.

1. **Who are these sentences about?**
   - ○ only Ben Wright
   - ● Ben Wright, his brother, and his dad
2. **Ben Wright, his brother, and his dad are** the Wright family.
   - ○ three school friends
   - ○ three cool cats
   - ● the Wright family
3. **What is the main idea of the sentences?**
   - ○ The boys moved to the Bronx.
   - ● The Wright family moved to the Bronx.
   - ○ The Wright family packed their belongings.
4. **Write the main idea.** (Start with *The Wright family . . .*)
   The Wright family moved to the Bronx.
5. **Draw a picture of the main idea.**

20

©2009 Sopris West Educational Services. All Rights Reserved.

PROCEDURES

Demonstrate and guide practice, as needed.

1. **Main Idea: Selection Response—Specific Instructions** (Items 1–3)
   Have students read the sentences in the gray box. Then have students read the questions or sentence stem and fill in the bubble and/or blank with the correct answer. For Items 2 and 3, say something like:
   The main idea tells us who or what the sentences are about.
   It also tells us the most important . . . thing that is happening.
   Read Item 2. Say "blank" when you get to the blank. (Ben Wright, his brother, and his dad . . .)
   We're going to figure out what Ben, his brother, and his dad are.
   Read the first choice. (Ben Wright, his brother, and his dad are three school friends.) Are they three school friends? (no) Does that make sense? (no)
   Repeat with the remaining choices.

   Read Item 3. (What is the main idea of the sentences?)
   Read the first choice. (The boys moved to the Bronx.) Is that what the sentences told us? (no)
   The boys didn't move by themselves, did they? (no) So that choice is not quite right.
   Repeat with the two remaining choices. Discuss why the second choice is the best one.

2. **Main Idea: Sentence Writing, Illustrating—Basic Instructions** (Items 4, 5)
   Have students start with the topic and write the main idea. Then have students visualize how to illustrate the main idea. Say something like:
   The main idea is "The Wright family moved to the Bronx." When I think about this sentence, I see all three Wrights carrying boxes. That's what I'm going to draw to illustrate the main idea.

❶ SOUND REVIEW

Use selected Sound Cards from Units 1 and 2.

❷ SHIFTY WORD BLENDING

For each word, have students say the underlined sound. Then have them sound out the word smoothly and say it. Use the words in sentences, as needed.

❸ ACCURACY AND FLUENCY BUILDING

- For each task, have students say any underlined part, then read the word.
- Set a pace. Then have students read the whole words in each task and column.
- Provide repeated practice, building accuracy first, then fluency.

A2. Names

For words that students may be able to sound out, have students figure out the word, then put their thumbs up when they know the word.

D1. Word Endings

Have students read the underlined word, then the word with an ending.

E1. Tricky Words

- For each Tricky Word, have students identify known sounds or word parts. Use the word in a sentence to help with pronunciation.
- If the word is unfamiliar, tell students the word. Then have students say, spell, and say it.

super
Look at the first word. Say the word by parts with me. su-per
Your idea is great. It is . . . *super.* Spell *super.* (s-u-p-e-r)
Read the word four times. (super, super, super, super)

brought
Look at the next word. That word is *brought.* Say the word. (brought)
Angela forgot to bring the equipment, so Tammy . . . *brought* . . . it. Spell *brought.* (b-r-o-u-g-h-t)
Say the word three times. (brought, brought, brought)

ocean	Sharks live in the . . . *ocean.*
answer	The teacher asked a question, but nobody had the . . . *answer.*
front	Don't sit in the back. Sit in the . . . *front.*
ideas	Inventors come up with new . . . *ideas.*

E2. Compound Words

- Remind students that compound words have two small words in one big word.
- For each word, have students read each small word, then read the compound word.

❹ MULTISYLLABIC WORDS

For each word, have students read each syllable, then read the whole word. Use the word in a sentence, as appropriate.

❺ PHRASES AND SENTENCES

Have students read each phrase and sentence, first for accuracy and then for fluency.

People on the Move

Unit 2 Exercise 5

Use before Chapter 3

1. SOUND REVIEW Use selected Sound Cards from Units 1 and 2.

2. SHIFTY WORD BLENDING For each word, have students say the underlined part, sound out smoothly, then read the word.

them	then	when	pen

3. ACCURACY AND FLUENCY BUILDING For each column, have students say any underlined part, then read each word. Next, have students read the whole column.

A1 Mixed Practice	B1 Bossy E	C1 Reading by Analogy	D1 Word Endings	E1 Tricky Words
bent	slave	me	clutching	super
shawl	trade	be	counted	brought
straw	fade	became	added	ocean
A2 Names	drive		fingers	answer
Betsy	**B2** Bossy E With Endings	no	**D2** Morphographs & Affixes	front
Alison	stolen	go	replay	ideas
Jason	traders	o-	rewrite	pulled
Emily	write	open	action	great
Mama	writing	opened	tradition	**E2** Compound Words
		over		cowboy
				granddad
				something

4. MULTISYLLABIC WORDS Have students read each word part, then read each whole word.

A	wood•en	wooden	wool•en	woolen
B	cat•tle	cattle	peb•ble	pebble
C	but•ton	button	care•ful•ly	carefully
D	pur•ple	purple	ban•da•na	bandana
E	ques•tions	questions	Af•ri•ca	Africa
F	in•ter•est•ing	interesting	ab•so•lute•ly	absolutely

5. PHRASES AND SENTENCES Have students read each row for accuracy, then fluency.

A	all of the kids / in Mr. Chapman's class / brought something / to share
B	All of the kids in Mr. Chapman's class brought something.
C	All of the kids in Mr. Chapman's class brought something to share.

14

TEACHING TO MASTERY/ DISCRIMINATION PRACTICE

Repeated Practice

Provide repeated practice on each task. If you hear an error, gently correct the whole group with a demonstration and/or guided practice. Move to another skill or task, then return to the difficult item many times—mixing group and individual turns, independent of your voice. When a task is easy, build speed of recognition.

Remember, practice makes perfect! And practice builds fluency.

CHAPTER 3 INSTRUCTIONS

Students read with the teacher.

COMPREHENSION PROCESSES

Remember, Understand, Apply, Evaluate

PROCEDURES

1. Reviewing Chapters 1 and 2

Identifying—What; Defining and Using Vocabulary—immigrant; Making Judgments

Review Chapters 1 and 2. Say something like:

We've been reading about how people move from place to place.

What are some reasons people move? (They move to start a new job, or to be near family, or for adventure. Early people moved to find food.)

What is an immigrant? (An immigrant is a person who moves to a new country.)

Do you think it would be easy or hard to immigrate? Why?

Why would it be bittersweet? (It would be hard to leave home, but fun to live in a new place and make new friends.)

2. Introducing Chapter 3

Identifying—Title

Say something like:

What's the title of Chapter 3? (Maya's Story) I wonder if Maya is going to move too.

3. First Reading

- Ask questions and discuss the story as indicated by the gray text.
- Mix group and individual turns, independent of your voice. Have students work toward a group accuracy goal of 0–3 errors.
- After reading the story, practice any difficult words. Reread the story if students have not reached the accuracy goal.

CORRECTING DECODING ERRORS

During story reading, gently correct any error, then have students reread the sentence.

4. Second Reading, Short Passage Practice: Developing Prosody

- Demonstrate expressive, fluent reading on the first paragraph. Read at a rate slightly faster than the students' rate. Say something like:

  Listen to my expression as I read the first paragraph. I'm going to pretend I'm telling you the story, so I want to make it sound as interesting as I can.

  "Maya Martinez stood in front of the class clutching a small wooden box. 'I have . . . '"

- Guide practice with your voice.
- Provide individual turns while others track with their fingers and whisper read.
- Repeat with one paragraph or one page at a time.

5. Whisper Reading: Repeated Reading

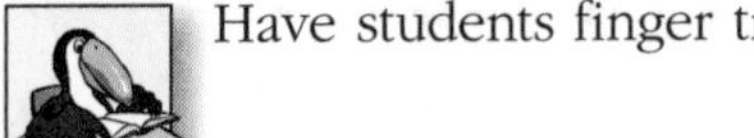

Have students finger track and whisper read before beginning independent work.

6. Homework 5: Repeated Reading

Maya's Story

Maya is going to tell a story about her family's history. Family histories almost always involve a . . . move.

Maya Martinez stood in front of the class clutching a small wooden box. "I have something very cool from my great-great-great-great-great-granddad," Maya said as she carefully counted the "greats" on her fingers.

Maya slowly opened the box. The class was absolutely still. Maya pulled out a faded red bandana. "My super-great-granddad was a cowboy," said Maya. Then she added, "This is his bandana. It is old, old, old.

"Mama says my super-great-granddad was a slave. His father was stolen from Africa. They put him in a big boat and brought him across the ocean. I don't think my super-great-granddad's father wanted to come. The slave traders made him move."

Maya said that her super-great-granddad's father was brought here from Africa. How did he get to the United States?[1] Was it right for the slave traders to steal him from Africa?[2] Maya has an interesting family story.

53

COMPREHENDING AS YOU GO

1 **Remember:** Identifying—How (He was put on a boat and sent across the ocean.)

2 **Evaluate:** Making Judgments (No, slavery is wrong . . .)

"When my super-great-granddad became a free man, he was very happy. He became a cowboy. I'm going to write my story about the bandana and how my super-great-granddad went on a cattle drive."

The class asked Maya questions. Maya wasn't sure how to answer many of them, but she got a lot of ideas for her story.

All of the kids in Mr. Chapman's class had brought something to write about. Emily had a purple button, Jason had a pebble, Alison had a bent straw, and Betsy had an old woolen shawl. Soon everyone was busy drawing and writing. There would be many interesting stories to read.

Why do you think Maya's super-great-granddad was happy being a cowboy?[1]
Do you have something that used to belong to your parents or grandparents?[2]
What does it tell you about your *relatives*?[3]

COMPREHENDING AS YOU GO

❶ **Apply:** Inferring (He was happy because he was free . . .)
❷ **Apply:** Making Connections (yes . . .)
❸ **Apply:** Inferring; Explaining; Using Vocabulary—relative (My relatives used to live in Ireland . . .)

CHARACTERIZATION

COMPREHENSION PROCESSES

Remember, Understand, Apply, Evaluate

WRITING TRAITS

Conventions—Complete Sentence, Capital, Period

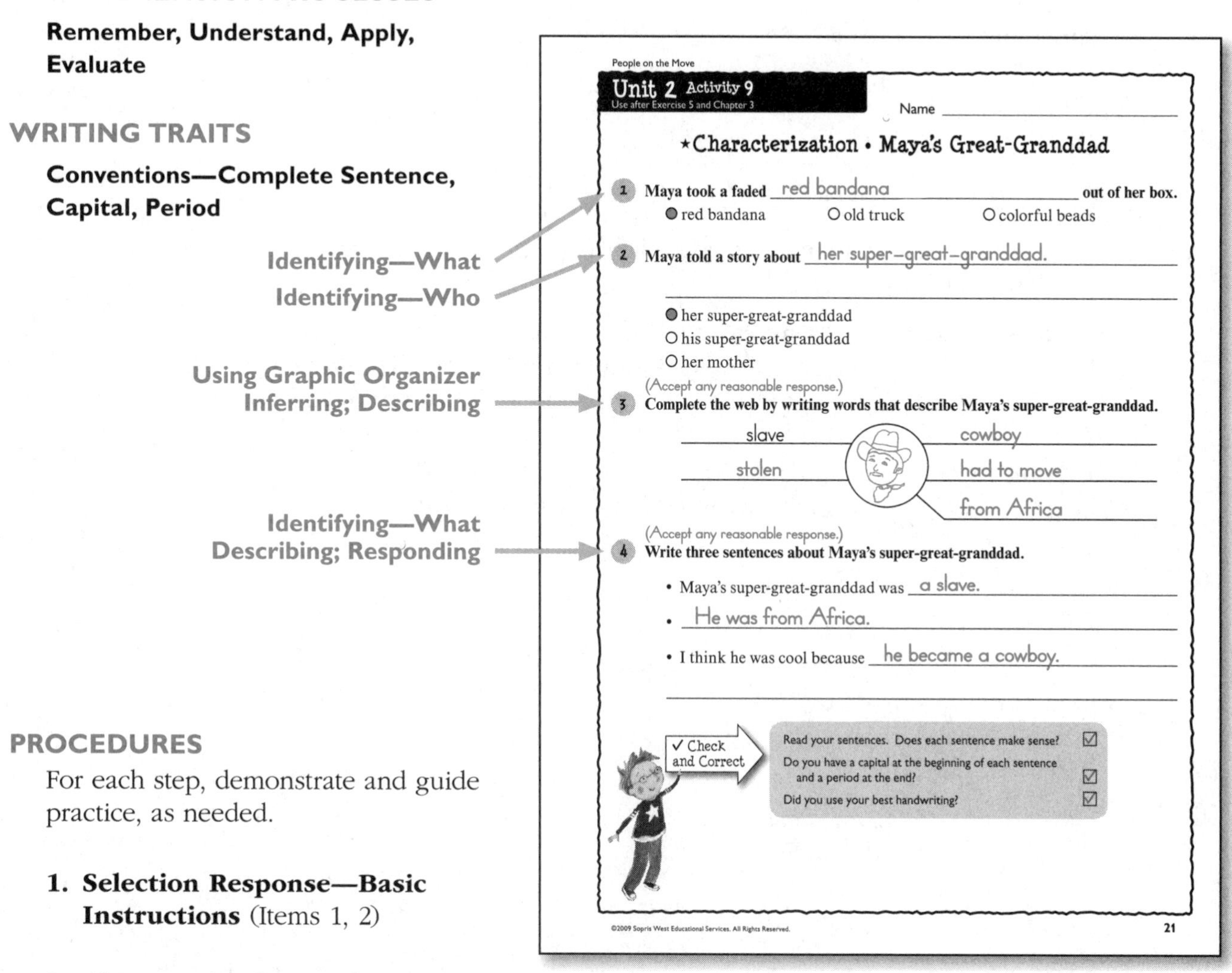

People on the Move

Unit 2 Activity 9
Use after Exercise 5 and Chapter 3

Name ______________________

★Characterization • Maya's Great-Granddad

1. **Maya took a faded** red bandana **out of her box.**
   - ● red bandana ○ old truck ○ colorful beads

2. **Maya told a story about** her super-great-granddad.
   - ● her super-great-granddad
   - ○ his super-great-granddad
   - ○ her mother

(Accept any reasonable response.)

3. **Complete the web by writing words that describe Maya's super-great-granddad.**
   - slave
   - stolen
   - cowboy
   - had to move
   - from Africa

(Accept any reasonable response.)

4. **Write three sentences about Maya's super-great-granddad.**
   - Maya's super-great-granddad was a slave.
   - He was from Africa.
   - I think he was cool because he became a cowboy.

✓ Check and Correct

- Read your sentences. Does each sentence make sense? ☑
- Do you have a capital at the beginning of each sentence and a period at the end? ☑
- Did you use your best handwriting? ☑

©2009 Sopris West Educational Services. All Rights Reserved. 21

PROCEDURES

For each step, demonstrate and guide practice, as needed.

1. **Selection Response—Basic Instructions** (Items 1, 2)

2. **Characterization: Web—Basic Instructions** (Item 3)

   Have students read the direction, brainstorm, and write descriptions.

   You're going to fill in a character web like we did in our Focus Lesson. When we describe a character, we use words that tell about the character. We're going to use a web to tell about Maya's super-great-granddad.

3. **Sentence Completion/Writing—Specific Instructions** (Item 4)
   - For the first two bullets, have students read the direction, brainstorm, then complete and/or write sentences.

     You're going to use your web to write three sentences about Maya's super-great-granddad. Read the first sentence starter. (Maya's super-great-granddad was . . .)
     Use some of the words from your web to complete the sentence. (Maya's super-great-granddad was a cowboy. Maya's super-great-granddad wore a bandana . . .)
     Use words from your web to complete the first sentence. Next, write a sentence of your own.
   - For the third bullet, have students brainstorm why they think Maya's super-great-granddad was cool. Then have them complete the sentence. Say something like:

     The last sentence starts with, "I think he was cool because . . . " I think Maya's super-great-granddad was cool because he went on cattle drives. Why do you think he was cool?

★VOCABULARY

COMPREHENSION PROCESSES

Remember, Understand

WRITING TRAITS

Conventions—Period

PROCEDURES

For each step, demonstrate and guide practice, as needed. Then have students complete the page independently.

Selection Response—Basic Instructions (Items 1–5)
Have students read each sentence, then fill in the bubble and blank with the correct vocabulary word. Remind students to put a period at the end of sentences.

Self-monitoring
Have students read their sentences to see if they make sense.

★= New in this unit

People on the Move

Unit 2 Activity 10
Use after Exercise 5 and Chapter 3

Name ______

★Vocabulary

Fill in the bubble for the correct word and write the word in the blank.

Defining and Using Vocabulary—cram, globe, immigrant

1. **To pick a place to move, my family looked at a map shaped like a ball.** We looked at a globe.
   - ○ cram ● globe ○ immigrant

Using Vocabulary—belongings, relative, tradition

2. **When we were ready to move, we packed our** belongings.
   - ● belongings ○ relatives ○ traditions

Using Vocabulary—vast, pout, cram

3. **To get all of my clothes into a small suitcase, I had to** cram **them in.**
   - ○ vast ○ pout ● cram

Using Vocabulary—continent, neighborhood, planet

4. **We said goodbye to the people who live and work near us. We said goodbye to everyone in our** neighborhood.
   - ○ continent ● neighborhood ○ planet

Using Vocabulary—immigrant, belongings, inventor

5. **We are moving to a new country. When we get to our new home, we will be** immigrants.
   - ● immigrants ○ belongings ○ inventors

22

1 SOUND REVIEW

Have students read the sounds and key word phrases. Work for accuracy, then fluency.

Read the sounds and the phrases. (/o͞o/ as in moon, /ōōō/ as in bone, /āāā/ as in hay, /aw/ as in paw)

2 SHIFTY WORD BLENDING

For each word, have students say the underlined sound. Then have them sound out the word smoothly and say it. Use the words in sentences, as needed.

3 SOUND PRACTICE

- For each task, have students spell and say the focus sound in the gray bar.
- Next, have students read each underlined sound, the word, then the whole column.
- Repeat with each column, building accuracy first, then fluency.

4 ACCURACY AND FLUENCY BUILDING

- For each task, have students say any underlined part, then read the word.
- Set a pace. Then have students read the whole words in each task and column.
- Provide repeated practice, building accuracy first, then fluency.

C1. Word Endings

Have students read the underlined word, then the word with an ending.
Note: For "win" and "hum," tell students you double the last letter when you add endings.

E1. Tricky Words

- For each Tricky Word, have students identify known sounds or word parts. Use the word in a sentence to help with pronunciation.
- If the word is unfamiliar, tell students the word. Then have students say, spell, and say it.

truly
Look at the first word. Say the word by parts with me. tru-ly
Sometimes we end our letters with "Yours . . . *truly*." Spell *truly*. (t-r-u-l-y)
Read the word two times. (truly, truly)

a-okay	The astronaut gave a thumbs up to let everyone know she was . . . *a-okay*.
poem	If you like poetry, you might like to read my . . . *poem*.
nothing	Shel didn't win anything. He got . . . *nothing*.
favorite	I like that shirt. It's my . . . *favorite*.

5 MULTISYLLABIC WORDS

For each word, have students read each syllable, finger count, then read the whole word. Use the word in a sentence, as appropriate.

yummy	2 syllables	That sweet watermelon was . . . *yummy*.
awesome	2 syllables	That sweet watermelon was . . . *awesome*.
corner	2 syllables	My sister was hiding just around the . . . *corner*.
muttering	3 syllables	I couldn't hear what Bo said because he was . . . *muttering*.
birthday	2 syllables	Cass will be eight years old on her . . . *birthday*.
absolutely	4 syllables	Are you sure? Are you . . . *absolutely* . . . positive?

6 PHRASES AND SENTENCES

Have students read each phrase and sentence, first for accuracy and then for fluency.

Fluency

Unit 2 Exercise 6

Use before That Kind of Day

1. SOUND REVIEW Have students review sounds for accuracy, then for fluency.

A	oo as in moon		o_e as in bone		ay as in hay	aw as in paw
B	ea	ow	i	wh	ch	er

2. SHIFTY WORD BLENDING For each word, have students say the underlined part, sound out smoothly, then read the word.

pink	pinch	punch	lunch	munch

ENTHUSIASM!
Small accomplishments become big accomplishments with your enthusiasm.

3. SOUND PRACTICE In each column, have students spell and say the sound, then say any underlined sound and the word. Next, have students read the whole column.

aw	all	ai	or	ir
saw	call	plain	sort	dirt
lawn	fall	mail	form	shirt
awful	small	e-mail	torn	girls

4. ACCURACY AND FLUENCY BUILDING For each column, have students say any underlined part, then read each word. Next, have students read the whole column.

A1 Bossy E	B1 Affixes	C1 Word Endings	D1 Story Words	E1 Tricky Words
game	-tion	drooling	face	truly
mine	action	shocking	goal	a-okay
wrote	question	stained	true	poem
fine	fiction	stomped		nothing
bones	tradition	winning		favorite
		hummed		

5. MULTISYLLABIC WORDS Have students read and finger count each word part, then read each whole word.

A	yum•my	yummy	aw~~e~~•some	awesome
B	cor•ner	corner	mut•ter•ing	muttering
C	birth•day	birthday	ab•so•lute•ly	absolutely

6. PHRASES AND SENTENCES Have students read each row for accuracy, then fluency.

A	Mighty Maya stomped around the apartment and muttered to herself
B	Mighty Maya stomped around the apartment.
C	Mighty Maya stomped around the apartment and muttered to herself.

FLUENCY PASSAGE INSTRUCTIONS

This Story Reading targets fluency as the primary goal of instruction and practice. Students do repeated readings of this short passage to improve accuracy, expression, and rate. Two poems are embedded in the narrative.

COMPREHENSION PROCESSES

Remember, Understand

PROCEDURES

1. **Warm-Up: Partner or Whisper Reading**

   Before beginning group Story Reading, have students finger track and partner or whisper read the selection.

2. **First Reading**
   - Mix group and individual turns, independent of your voice. Have students work toward a group accuracy goal of 0–4 errors. Quietly keep track of errors made by all students in the group.
   - After reading the story, practice any difficult words. Reread the story if students have not reached the accuracy goal.

3. **Second Reading, Short Passage Practice: Developing Prosody**
   - Demonstrate reading the first paragraph with expression and fluency. Have students finger track as you read.
   - Have students choral read the first paragraph. Encourage reading with expression and fluency.
   - Repeat with second paragraph.

4. **Third Reading, Timed Readings: Repeated Reading**

   - Select a page. Encourage each child to work for a personal best. Have students whisper read for a one-minute Timed Reading. Tell students to go back to the top of the page and keep reading until the minute is up.
   - Have students put their finger on the last word they read and count the number of words read correctly in one minute.
   - Have students do a second Timed Reading of the same page.
   - Have students try to beat their last score.
   - Celebrate improvements.

5. **Comprehension and Skill**

   Tell students they will do Comprehension and Skill Activities 11 and 12 after they read the poem on their own. Guide practice, as needed. For teacher directions, see pages 76 and 77 in this guide.

6. **Homework 6: Repeated Reading**

WITH THE TEACHER

Fluency

That Kind of Day

by Jessica Sprick and Ms. Mak
illustrated by Jana Christy

It was a perfect year, until Maya got an e-mail from her friend Ben. Maya stomped around the apartment, muttering to herself. Then she sat down and wrote a poem.

A Yucky, Yucky Day

It's been that kind of day, 6
A yucky sort of day. 11
Nothing, absolutely nothing, 14
Nothing's gone my way! 18

Got mud on my new shirt, 24
I stained my birthday shirt. 29
Awful, absolutely awful, 32
As bad as eating dirt! 37

Mom packed a yummy lunch, 42
My favorite-ever lunch. 46
Yucky, absolutely yucky, 49
To find a bug to munch! 55

55

FOCUS ON GENRE
Classifying
After reading the first part of the poem, say something like:
"A Yucky, Yucky Day" has short lines and a little rhythm. It isn't a story. What is it? (a poem)
That's right. It has short lines and a little rhythm. This poem also has a lot of rhyming words. Let's read the poem again, just for fun. Remember to read it with expression. After all, what kind of day is it about? (a yucky day) Why is it a yucky day? (Maya got mud on her birthday shirt and found a bug in her lunch. Yuck!)

WITH THE TEACHER

Fluency

The soccer game was on,	5
The kick was mine or gone.	11
Shocking, absolutely shocking,	14
To find my face on the lawn!	21
My bestest friend is Ben,	26
Funny, just plain Ben.	30
Awful, absolutely awful,	33
He's on the move again!	38
It's been that kind of day,	44
A yucky sort of day.	49
Nothing, absolutely nothing,	52
Nothing's gone my way.	56

Two weeks passed. Maya wrote a cool story about her super-great-grandfather. She got an A++. Maya hummed. Then she sat down and wrote a new poem.

56

FOCUS ON COMPREHENSION

Explaining

After reading the second part of the poem, say something like:

Maya's certainly having a . . . yucky day. She got mud on her birthday shirt and found a bug in her lunch. What else made it a yucky day? (She fell during the soccer game, her best friend Ben is moving . . . nothing is going right.)

An Almost Perfect Day

It's an a-okay day, 5
An almost perfect day. 9
Many things, a lot of things, 15
Have really gone my way! 20

Mom packed a yummy lunch, 25
My bestest-ever lunch. 29
Yummy, truly yummy, 32
Drooling as I munch! 36

The corner kick was fine, 41
A soccer game so fine. 46
Perfect, truly perfect, 49
That winning goal was mine! 54

An e-mail from pal Ben, 59
Funny, just plain Ben. 63
Awesome, really awesome, 66
Bones from way back when! 71

It's been a super day, 76
An almost perfect day. 80
Many things, a lot of things, 86
Have really gone my way! 91

FOCUS ON COMPREHENSION

Explaining

After reading "An Almost Perfect Day," say something like:
Things have changed for Maya. What's better now? (She had a yummy lunch. She kicked a winning goal. She got an e-mail from Ben.)

CHARACTERIZATION

COMPREHENSION PROCESSES

Understand, Apply, Create

WRITING TRAITS

Conventions—Complete Sentence, Capital, Period

Describing; Illustrating Using Graphic Organizer

Describing, Generating Ideas

PREP NOTE

To demonstrate, use an overhead of page 23 from *Activity Book 1*, write on a transparency placed over the page, or use a paper copy.

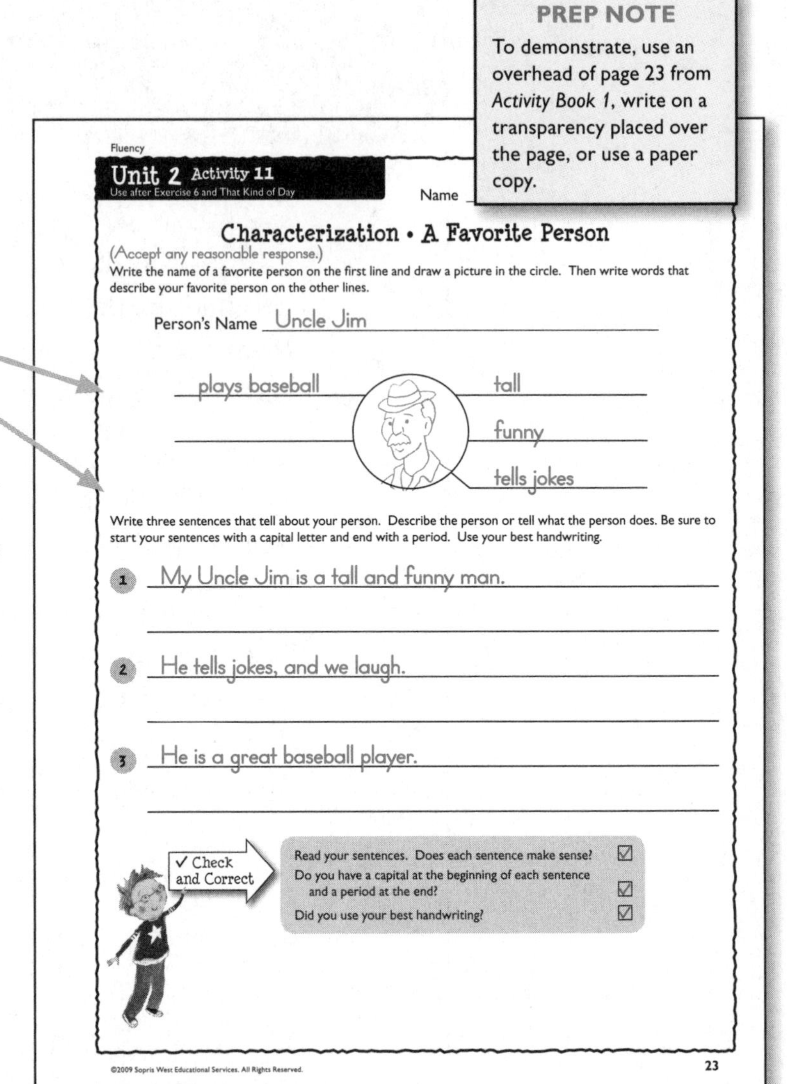

Fluency

Unit 2 Activity 11
Use after Exercise 6 and That Kind of Day

Name

Characterization • A Favorite Person

(Accept any reasonable response.)

Write the name of a favorite person on the first line and draw a picture in the circle. Then write words that describe your favorite person on the other lines.

Person's Name Uncle Jim

plays baseball

tall

funny

tells jokes

Write three sentences that tell about your person. Describe the person or tell what the person does. Be sure to start your sentences with a capital letter and end with a period. Use your best handwriting.

1. My Uncle Jim is a tall and funny man.
2. He tells jokes, and we laugh.
3. He is a great baseball player.

✓ Check and Correct

Read your sentences. Does each sentence make sense? ☑

Do you have a capital at the beginning of each sentence and a period at the end? ☑

Did you use your best handwriting? ☑

©2009 Sopris West Educational Services. All Rights Reserved.

23

PROCEDURES

For each step, demonstrate and guide practice, as needed. Then have students complete the page independently.

1. Characterization: Web—Specific Instructions

- Have students brainstorm names of some of their favorite people.
  You're going to complete a character web about a favorite person. Favorite people are people you like a lot. They are very special and fun to be with. Who are some of your favorite people? (Grandma, Uncle Joe, Beth . . .) My favorite person is Grandpa Jon.
- Have students write the person's name in the blank and draw that person's picture in the circle.
  Write your favorite person's name on the line. Later, you will draw a picture of that person in the circle. I am going to write Grandpa Jon on the line.
- Have students write descriptions of their person in the blanks.
  What makes your favorite person special? Write words that describe your favorite person on the lines. Grandpa Jon likes to play checkers with me, he tells funny stories, and he is a great cook. So I'm going to write "plays checkers," "tells funny stories," and "great cook" on the lines.

2. Sentence Writing—Specific Instructions

Have students write three sentences about their person.

Now you're going to write three complete sentences that tell about your favorite person. The sentences should describe the person or tell what he or she does. Use your web to help you.

I can write that Grandpa Jon is a great cook. Be sure to write a complete sentence. Start with a capital and end with a period.

Self-monitoring

Demonstrate how to use the Check and Correct box to self-monitor. Remind students that the Check and Correct box will help them do their personal best.

TABLE OF CONTENTS AND FOLLOWING DIRECTIONS

COMPREHENSION PROCESSES

Understand

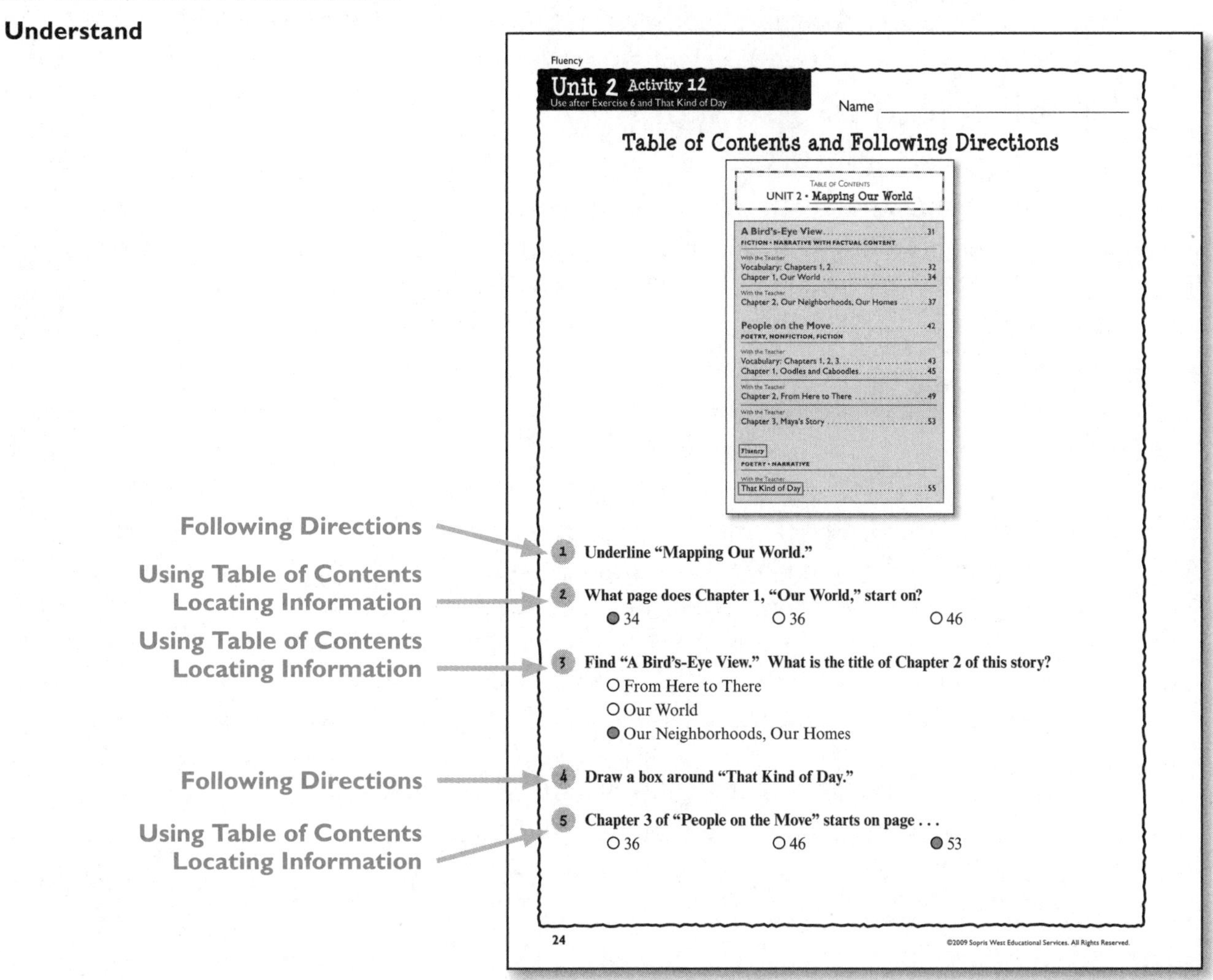

Fluency

Unit 2 Activity 12
Use after Exercise 6 and That Kind of Day

Name ____________________

Table of Contents and Following Directions

Table of Contents
UNIT 2 • Mapping Our World

1. **Underline "Mapping Our World."**
2. **What page does Chapter 1, "Our World," start on?**
   ● 34 ○ 36 ○ 46
3. **Find "A Bird's-Eye View." What is the title of Chapter 2 of this story?**
   ○ From Here to There
   ○ Our World
   ● Our Neighborhoods, Our Homes
4. **Draw a box around "That Kind of Day."**
5. **Chapter 3 of "People on the Move" starts on page . . .**
   ○ 36 ○ 46 ● 53

24

PROCEDURES

For each step, demonstrate and guide practice, as needed. Then have students complete the page independently.

1. **Following Directions—Specific Instructions** (Items 1, 4)
   Have students look at the Table of Contents and follow the specific directions.

2. **Table of Contents: Selection Response—Basic Instructions** (Items 2, 3, 5)
   - Have students read each sentence or question, then fill in the bubble with the correct answer.
   - Think aloud with students and discuss the multiple-choice options, as needed.

Self-monitoring

Have students check and correct their work.

End of the Unit

In this section, you will find:

Making Decisions

As you near the end of the unit, plan to give the Oral Reading Fluency Assessment to each child in your group. Use this section as a general guide for making instructional decisions and doing diagnostic planning.

Oral Reading Fluency Assessment

The Unit 2 Oral Reading Fluency Assessment is located on page 81 of this teacher's guide and in the *Assessment Manual.*

Certificate of Achievement and Goal Setting

Celebrate your children's accomplishments. When your students master the unit skills, send home the Certificate of Achievement. Have students set goals for the next unit.

Extra Practice Lessons

Use the Extra Practice lessons for students who need additional decoding and fluency work. Student materials can be copied from the Extra Practice blackline masters.

Making Decisions

USING THE ORAL READING FLUENCY RESULTS

At the end of each unit, you will need to make decisions regarding student progress. Should students go forward in the program? Does the group need Extra Practice before proceeding? Do individuals require more assistance and practice to continue working in their group? These decisions all require use of the oral reading fluency data and professional judgment. As you analyze assessment results, watch for trends and anomalies.

See the *Assessment Manual* for detailed information and instructional recommendations. General guidelines and recommendations follow:

Strong Pass ≥ 101 WCPM 0–2 errors	• Continue with the current pace of instruction. • Have students set goals. (Until students are reading approximately 180 words correct per minute, oral reading fluency continues to be an instructional goal.)
Pass 80–100 WCPM 0–2 errors	• Continue with the current pace of instruction. Consider increasing fluency practice.
No Pass ≤ 79 WCPM	• If a child scores a No Pass but has previously passed all assessments, you may wish to advance the student to the next unit, then carefully monitor the student. • If a child scores a No Pass but has previously passed all assessments, you may wish to advance the student to the next unit and also provide additional practice opportunities. (See below.) • If a child scores two consecutive No Passes or periodic No Passes, additional practice must be provided. (See below.) • If a child scores three consecutive No Passes, the student should be placed in a lower-performing group.

RED FLAG

A No Pass is a red flag. A mild early intervention can prevent an intense and time-consuming intervention in the future.

Added Practice Options for Groups

Warm-Ups: Begin each story reading with a review of the previous day's story. After reading the story, include Short Passage Practice on a daily basis.

Extended Units: If several children begin to score No Passes or barely pass, consider extending the unit by adding Extra Practice Lessons 1, 2, and/or 3. Extra Practice lessons include Decoding Practice, Passage Fluency, and a Comprehension and Skill Activity. (See pages 83 to 94 in this guide.)

Vowel Review: Consider a review of selected vowel units from *Read Well 1* or *Fluency Foundations.*

Added Practice Options for Individual Students

Tutorials: Set up five-minute tutorials on a daily basis with an assistant, trained volunteer, or cross-age tutor. Have the tutor provide Short Passage Practice and Timed Readings or Extra Practice lessons.

Double Dose: Find ways to provide a double dose of *Read Well* instruction:

- Have the student work in his or her group *and* a lower-performing group.
- Have an instructional assistant, older student, or parent volunteer preview or review lessons.
- Have an instructional assistant provide instruction with Extra Practice lessons.

END-OF-THE-UNIT CELEBRATION

When students pass the Oral Reading Fluency Assessment, celebrate with the Certificate of Achievement on page 82.

Note: Using the Flesch-Kincaid Grade Level readability formula, the Unit 2 Assessment has a 2.4 readability level. Readabilities are based on number of words per sentence and number of syllables per word. Adding one or two multisyllabic words can increase readability by a month or two. Though we are attending to readability for the assessments, the overriding factor is decodability.

GOAL SETTING

If you choose to do goal setting with students, help them brainstorm accomplishments in reading.

Say something like:

Let's look at our goal-setting form.
It starts with "I am proud because I . . . "

Goal Setting

I am proud because I met my goal.
My goal is to read one word per minute faster.
I will work on my goal by:

- Reading and rereading carefully
- Working hard in reading group
- Reading my homework

Signed Jason
Date Sept. 22

My Personal Best:
In this unit, my fluency was 81.
My personal best is 85 words correct per minute.

82 Blackline Master

I'm proud of you because you completed all of your homework!
What are some other things you are proud of?
(meeting my accuracy goal . . .)

That's a great accomplishment.
It is something to be proud of!
Please complete the sentence, "I am proud because I . . . "

The next line says, "My goal is to . . . "
For Unit 3, I'd like all of you to work on increasing your reading fluency by one word per minute. What does your goal say? (My goal is to read one word per minute faster.)

The next line says, "I will work on my goal by . . . "
Everyone, read what you will do to reach your goal.
(Reading and rereading carefully, working hard in reading group . . .)

[Jason], what will you do to improve your reading fluency? (Read my homework stories.)

The next part of your form tells you what your fluency was for Unit 2. It also tells you what your personal best is. Please whisper read the sentence that begins, "In this unit . . . "
I think everyone is going to meet their goals for Unit 3!

TRICKY WORD and FOCUS SKILL WARM-UP

friends	wanted	mother	ordinary	awesome	father

ORAL READING FLUENCY PASSAGE

A Birthday Surprise

★Today was not an ordinary day for Maya. It was her	11
birthday! Maya's mom said she could play with her best friends	22
all day.	24
Maya looked out at the dark clouds. Rain began to fall.	35
"Oh, no," said Maya. "This is awful!"	42
Maya didn't want it to rain on her birthday. She wanted it	54
to be sunny so she could play with her friends outside.	65
Maya's mother said, "Don't be sad. It will stop raining	75
soon."	76
Maya waited. Her friends came. They had a lot of fun	87
drawing pictures. They played games and they ate birthday cake.	97
The sun came out. Everyone went outside and shouted "Happy	107
birthday. Happy birthday!"	110
Maya smiled. Then she saw her grandfather. "Awesome!	118
You came!" said Maya. "What a perfect birthday." Granddad	127
gave Maya a big hug.	132

ORAL READING FLUENCY Start timing at the ★. Mark errors. Make a single slash in the text (/) at 60 seconds. Have the student complete the passage. If the student completes the passage in less than 60 seconds, have the student go back to the ★and continue reading. Make a double slash (//) in the text at 60 seconds.

WCPM Determine words correct per minute by subtracting errors from words read in 60 seconds.

STRONG PASS The student scores no more than 2 errors on the first pass through the passage and reads 101 or more words correct per minute. Proceed to Unit 3.

PASS The student scores no more than 2 errors on the first pass through the passage and reads 80 to 100 words correct per minute. Proceed to Unit 3.

NO PASS The student scores 3 or more errors on the first pass through the passage and/or reads 79 or fewer words correct per minute. Provide added fluency practice with *RW2* Unit 2 Extra Practice. (Lessons follow the certificate at the end of the teacher's guide). After completing the Extra Practice, retest the student.

Fantastic!

has successfully completed

Read Well* 2 Unit 2 • *Mapping Our World

with ______ words correct per minute.

Teacher Signature ______________________

Date ______________________

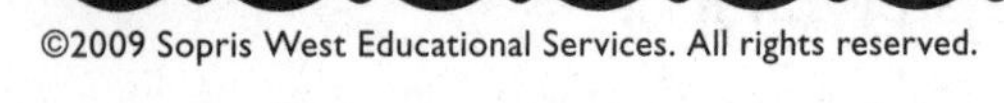

Fantastic!

has successfully completed

Read Well 2 Unit 2 • Mapping Our World

with ______ words correct per minute.

Teacher Signature ______________________

Date ______________________

Goal Setting

I am proud because I ______________________________

My goal is to ______________________________

I will work on my goal by:

- Reading and rereading carefully
- Working hard in reading group
- ______________________

Signed ______________________

Date ______________________

My Personal Best:

In this unit, my fluency was ______ .

My personal best is ______ words correct per minute.

Goal Setting

I am proud because I ______________________________

My goal is to ______________________________

I will work on my goal by:

- Reading and rereading carefully
- Working hard in reading group
- ______________________

Signed ______________________

Date ______________________

My Personal Best:

In this unit, my fluency was ______ .

My personal best is ______ words correct per minute.

PROCEDURES

1. Sound Review

Use selected Sound Cards from Units 1 and 2.

- Have students say each sound, building accuracy first, then fluency.
- Mix group and individual turns, independent of your voice.

2. Sounding Out Smoothly

- For each word, have students say the underlined part, sound out the word smoothly, then read the whole word. Use the words in sentences, as needed.
- Repeat practice.

3. Accuracy and Fluency Building

- For each task, have students say any underlined part, then read each word.
- Set a pace. Then have students read the whole words in each task and column.
- Provide repeated practice, building accuracy first, then fluency.

EXTRA PRACTICE 1

Unit 2 Decoding Practice

Name ____________________

1. SOUND REVIEW Use selected Sound Cards from Units 1 and 2.

2. SOUNDING OUT SMOOTHLY Have students say the underlined part, sound out and read each word, then read the row.

creek	ranch	still	chunk

3. ACCURACY/FLUENCY BUILDING Have students say any underlined part, then read each word. Next, have students read the column.

A1 Sound Practice	B1 Word Endings	C1 Rhyming Words	D1 Sound Practice
saw draw law	story stories	stood wood	about along around across
A2 Mixed Practice	stop stopped	fall tall small	**D2** Compound Words
right down ear found even	skip skipped hope hoped	told cold	everyone something outside

4. TRICKY WORDS Have students read each row for accuracy, then fluency.

A	many	water	pretty	are	through	5
B	again	sure	walked	wanted	pulled	10

5. MULTISYLLABIC WORDS Have students read the word by parts, tell how many syllables are in the word, then read the whole word.

A	crick•et	cricket	birth•day	birthday
B	let•ter	letter	fam•i•ly	family
C	slip•per•y	slippery	won•der•ful	wonderful

6. DICTATION Say the word. Have students say the word, then finger count and say the sounds. Have students say each sound as they touch or write it.

A1 Shifty Words	B1 Rhyming Words
th e m	sh a ck
th e n	b l a ck
wh e n	s n a ck

 10

4. Tricky Words

Have students read each row for accuracy, then fluency.

CAUTION

Your children may not need Extra Practice. Use assessment results to determine if Extra Practice is needed.

5. Multisyllabic Words

For each word, have students read each syllable out loud, finger count the syllables, then tell how many syllables are in the word. If needed, use the word in a sentence. Have students read the whole word.

6. Dictation

them, then, when, shack, black, snack

- Say "them." Have students say the word. Guide students as they finger count and say the sounds. Have students touch or write the sounds, then read the word. Say something like:

  The first word is ***them.*** Say the word. (them)

  Say and count the sounds in ***them*** with me.

  Hold up one finger for each sound. /ththth/•/ĕĕĕ/•/mmm/ How many sounds? (three)

  What's the first sound? (/ththth/) Touch under /ththth/.

  What's the next sound? (/ĕĕĕ/) Write /ĕĕĕ/.

  What's the last sound? (/mmm/) Touch under /mmm/. Read the word. (them)

- Repeat with "then" and "when."
- Continue with the rhyming words: shack, black, snack.

PROCEDURES

EXTRA PRACTICE 1

Unit 2 Fluency Passage

Name ______

Fluency Passage

My goal is to read with 0–2 errors and ___ words correct per minute.

I read with ___ errors and ___ words correct per minute.

Cricket Creek Ranch

Benjamin and Grandmother Molly walked through the tall trees	9
along the creek. Molly stopped and looked at her maps. "The maps	21
say that Cricket Creek Ranch was right here," she said.	31
Benjamin looked around. Not even an old shack still stood. "Are	42
you sure?"	44
Grandmother Molly looked at the map again. "Pretty sure."	53
Benjamin felt sad. Molly had told him many wonderful family	63
stories about the ranch. He had hoped to see something.	73
Then down by the creek, Benjamin saw a small chunk of wood. He	86
skipped down to the water and pulled the wood from the slippery mud.	99
"What is it?" asked Grandmother Molly.	105
Benjamin grinned from ear to ear. "It's the letter C. We found it!	118
Cricket Creek Ranch was right here."	124

Homework

I've listened to my child read this passage twice. Date ______ Signed ______

©2009 Sopris West Educational Services. All Rights Reserved.

11

1. **First Reading**
   Mix group and individual turns, independent of your voice. Have students work toward an accuracy goal of 0–2 errors and practice any difficult words.

2. **Second Reading, Short Passage Practice: Developing Prosody**
   - Demonstrate how to read a line or two with expression. Read at a rate slightly faster than the students' rate. Say something like:
     Listen as I read the first two sentences with expression and phrasing. I'm going to emphasize certain words and pause between sentences.

     "Benjamin and Grandma Molly walked through the tall trees along the creek. Molly stopped and looked at her maps."
   - Guide practice with your voice.
     Now read the paragraph with me.
   - Provide individual turns while others track with their fingers and whisper read. Provide descriptive, positive feedback.
     [Ricardo], you read with wonderful expression!

3. **Partner Reading: Repeated Reading (Checkout Opportunity)**

While students do Partner Reading, listen to individuals read the passage. Work on accuracy and fluency, as needed.

4. **Homework: Repeated Reading**

Have students read the story at home.

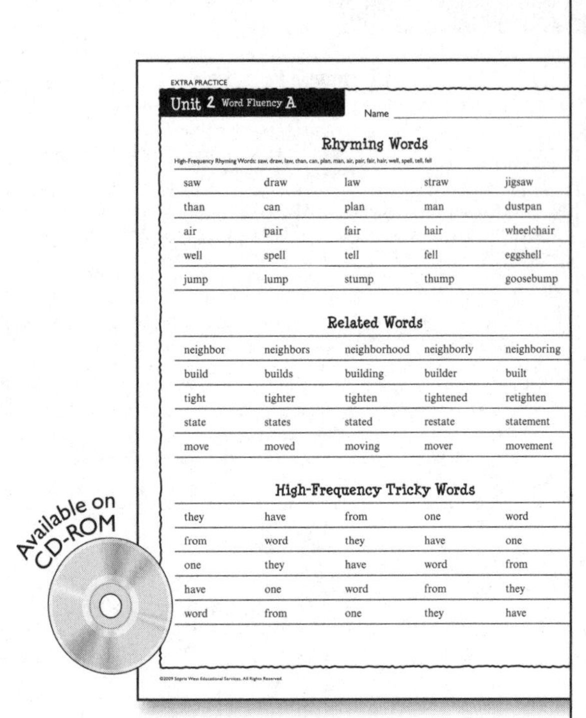

EXTRA PRACTICE

Unit 2 Word Fluency A

Name ____________

Rhyming Words

saw	draw	law	straw	jigsaw
than	can	plan	man	dustpan
air	pair	fair	hair	wheelchair
well	spell	tell	fell	eggshell
jump	lump	stump	thump	goosebump

Related Words

neighbor	neighbors	neighborhood	neighborly	neighboring
build	builds	building	builder	built
tight	tighter	tighten	tightened	retighten
state	states	stated	restate	statement
move	moved	moving	mover	movement

High-Frequency Tricky Words

they	have	from	one	word
from	word	they	have	one
one	they	have	word	from
have	one	word	from	they
word	from	one	they	have

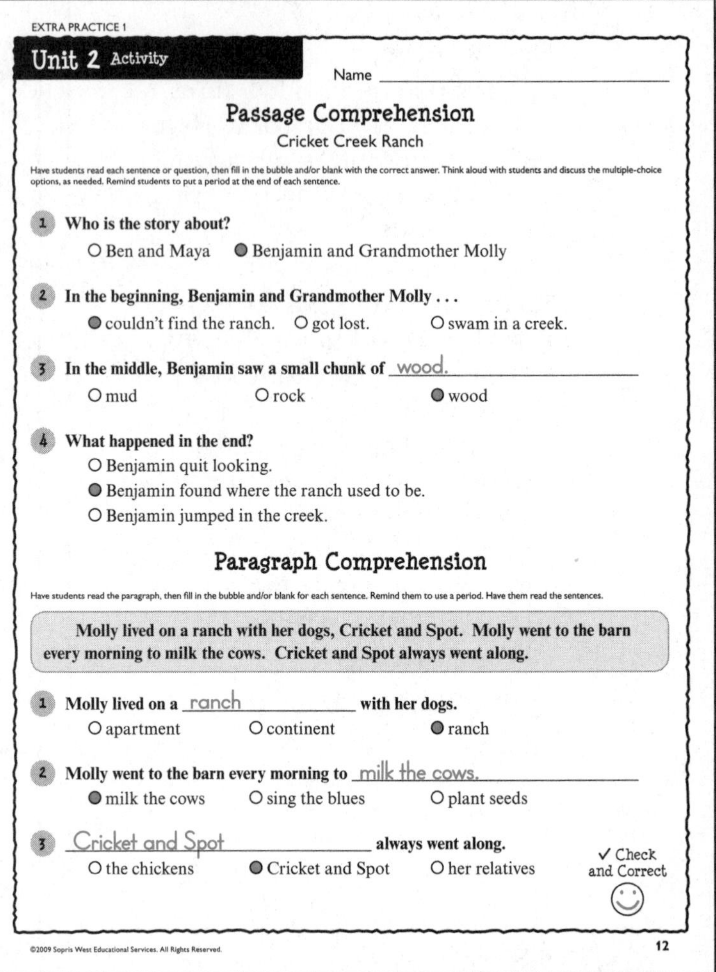

EXTRA PRACTICE 1

Unit 2 Activity

Name ____________

Passage Comprehension

Cricket Creek Ranch

Have students read each sentence or question, then fill in the bubble and/or blank with the correct answer. Think aloud with students and discuss the multiple-choice options, as needed. Remind students to put a period at the end of each sentence.

1. **Who is the story about?**
   ○ Ben and Maya ● Benjamin and Grandmother Molly
2. **In the beginning, Benjamin and Grandmother Molly . . .**
   ● couldn't find the ranch. ○ got lost. ○ swam in a creek.
3. **In the middle, Benjamin saw a small chunk of** wood.
   ○ mud ○ rock ● wood
4. **What happened in the end?**
   ○ Benjamin quit looking.
   ● Benjamin found where the ranch used to be.
   ○ Benjamin jumped in the creek.

Paragraph Comprehension

Have students read the paragraph, then fill in the bubble and/or blank for each sentence. Remind them to use a period. Have them read the sentences.

Molly lived on a ranch with her dogs, Cricket and Spot. Molly went to the barn every morning to milk the cows. Cricket and Spot always went along.

1. **Molly lived on a** ranch **with her dogs.**
   ○ apartment ○ continent ● ranch
2. **Molly went to the barn every morning to** milk the cows.
   ● milk the cows ○ sing the blues ○ plant seeds
3. Cricket and Spot **always went along.**
   ○ the chickens ● Cricket and Spot ○ her relatives

✓ Check and Correct

©2009 Sopris West Educational Services. All Rights Reserved. 12

PROCEDURES

For each step, demonstrate and guide practice, as needed. Then have students complete the page independently.

> **ACCURACY BEFORE FLUENCY**
> Word Fluency is designed to build accuracy and fluency. Students should practice for accuracy before working on fluency.

1. Activity

Passage Comprehension

- Have students read each sentence or phrase, then fill in the bubble and/or blank with the correct answer.
- Think aloud with students and discuss the multiple-choice options, as needed.
- Remind students to put a period at the end of sentences.

Paragraph Comprehension

- Have students read the paragraph.
- Have students read each numbered sentence or phrase, then fill in the bubble and/or blank. Remind them to end sentences with a period, where needed.
- Have students read the completed sentences.

Self-monitoring

Have students read and check their work, then draw a happy face in the circle.

2. Word Fluency (BLMs are located on the CD.)

- To build fluency, have students read Rhyming Words, Related Words, and High-Frequency Tricky Words. Have students read each section three times in a row.
- To build accuracy, have students read all sets with partners.

PROCEDURES

1. Sound Review

Use selected Sound Cards from Units 1 and 2.

- Have students say each sound, building accuracy first, then fluency.
- Mix group and individual turns.

2. Sounding Out Smoothly

- For each word, have students say the underlined part, sound out the word smoothly, then read the whole word. (Use the words in sentences, as needed.)
- Repeat practice.

3. Accuracy and Fluency Building

- For each task, have students say any underlined part, then read each word.
- Set a pace. Then have students read the whole words in each task and column.
- Provide repeated practice, building accuracy first, then fluency.

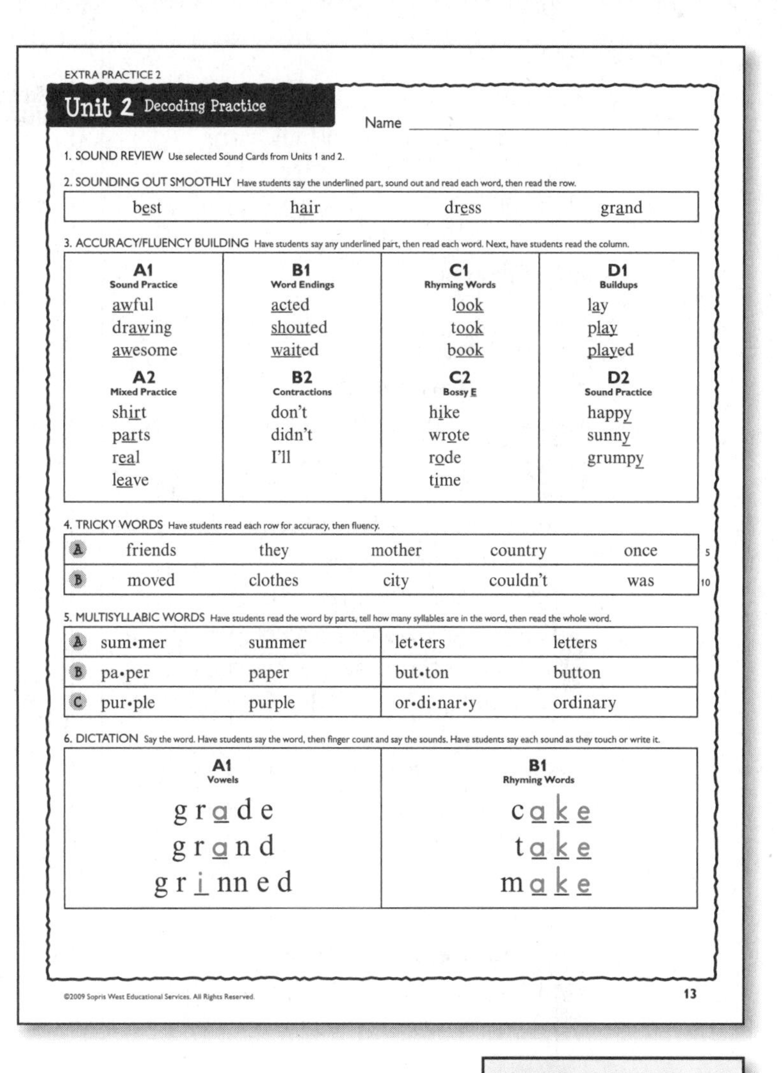

EXTRA PRACTICE 2

Unit 2 Decoding Practice

Name ____________________

1. SOUND REVIEW Use selected Sound Cards from Units 1 and 2.

2. SOUNDING OUT SMOOTHLY Have students say the underlined part, sound out and read each word, then read the row.

best	hair	dress	grand

3. ACCURACY/FLUENCY BUILDING Have students say any underlined part, then read each word. Next, have students read the column.

A1 Sound Practice	B1 Word Endings	C1 Rhyming Words	D1 Buildups
awful	acted	look	lay
drawing	shouted	took	play
awesome	waited	book	played
A2 Mixed Practice	**B2 Contractions**	**C2 Bossy E**	**D2 Sound Practice**
shirt	don't	hike	happy
parts	didn't	wrote	sunny
real	I'll	rode	grumpy
leave		time	

4. TRICKY WORDS Have students read each row for accuracy, then fluency.

A	friends	they	mother	country	once	5
B	moved	clothes	city	couldn't	was	10

5. MULTISYLLABIC WORDS Have students read the word by parts, tell how many syllables are in the word, then read the whole word.

A	sum•mer	summer	let•ters	letters
B	pa•per	paper	but•ton	button
C	pur•ple	purple	or•di•nar•y	ordinary

6. DICTATION Say the word. Have students say the word, then finger count and say the sounds. Have students say each sound as they touch or write it.

A1 Vowels	B1 Rhyming Words
g r a d e	c a k e
g r a n d	t a k e
g r i nn e d	m a k e

13

4. Tricky Words

Have students read each row for accuracy, then fluency.

CAUTION

Your children may not need Extra Practice. Use assessment results to determine if Extra Practice is needed.

5. Multisyllabic Words

For each word, have students read each syllable out loud, finger count the syllables, then tell how many syllables are in the word. If needed, use the word in a sentence. Have students read the whole word.

6. Dictation

grade, grand, grinned, cake, take, make

- Say "grade." Have students say the word. Guide students as they finger count and say the sounds. Have students touch or write the sounds, then read the word.

  The first word is ***grade***. Say the word. (grade) Say and count the sounds in ***grade*** with me.
  Hold up one finger for each sound. /g/•/rrr/•/āāā/•/d/ How many sounds? (four)
  What's the first sound? (/g/) Touch under /g/.
  What's the next sound? (/rrr/) Touch under /rrr/.
  What's the next sound? (/āāā/) Write /āāā/.
  What's the last sound? (/d/) Touch under /d/. Read the word. (grade)
  Yes, the Bossy E at the end makes letter a say its name.

- Repeat with "grand" and "grinned."
- Continue with the rhyming words: cake, take, make.

PROCEDURES

1. First Reading

Mix group and individual turns, independent of your voice. Have students work toward an accuracy goal of 0–2 errors and practice any difficult words.

2. Second Reading, Timed Reading: Repeated Reading

- Once the group accuracy goal has been achieved, time individual students for 30 or 60 seconds while the other children track with their fingers and whisper read.
- Determine words correct per minute. Record student scores. Celebrate when students reach their goals!

  Wow! [Nick], you met your goal. That was your best score ever. You get to read to the principal this week.

EXTRA PRACTICE 2

Unit 2 Fluency Passage

Name ____________________

Fluency Passage

My goal is to read with 0–2 errors and ___ words correct per minute.

I read with ___ errors and ___ words correct per minute.

The Purple Button

Emily's best friend, Ann, moved across the country. Ann dressed in purple clothes. She wrote letters to Emily on purple paper. Once she even had purple hair. 10 23 27

Last summer, Ann came to see Emily. They had a grand time. They played games and rode bikes. They made up plays and acted out all the parts. Emily's mother took them into the city to see a real play, and they dressed in the same purple clothes. 40 54 69 75

When it was time for Ann to leave, Emily was sad. So Ann took a button off her purple shirt and gave it to Emily. 90 100

"Now I'll have to come back next summer to get my button!" Ann said. Emily grinned. She couldn't wait. 113 119

Homework

I've listened to my child read this passage twice. Date ________ Signed ____________________

©2009 Sopris West Educational Services. All Rights Reserved.

14

3. Partner Reading: Repeated Reading (Checkout Opportunity)

While students do Partner Reading, listen to individuals read the passage. Work on accuracy and fluency, as needed.

4. Homework: Repeated Reading

Have students read the story at home.

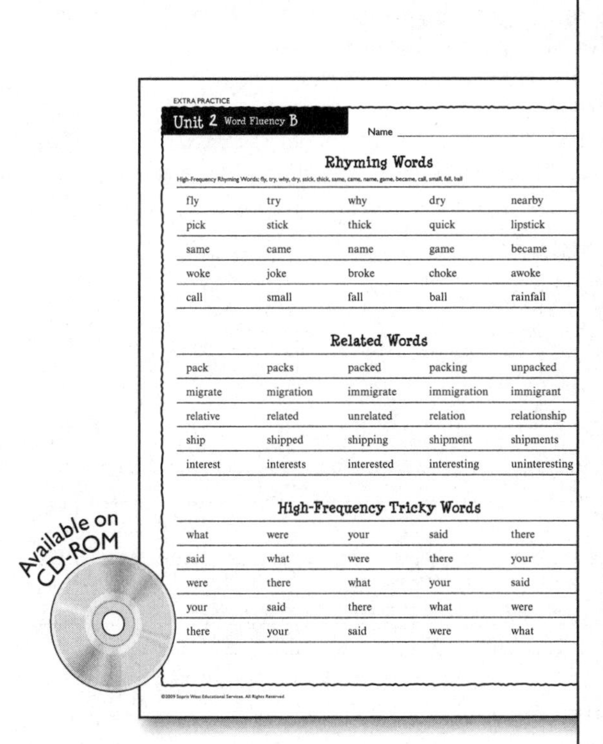

EXTRA PRACTICE

Unit 2 Word Fluency B

Name ______

Rhyming Words

High-Frequency Rhyming Words: fly, try, why, dry, stick, thick, same, came, name, game, became, call, small, fall, ball

fly	try	why	dry	nearby
pick	stick	thick	quick	lipstick
same	came	name	game	became
woke	joke	broke	choke	awoke
call	small	fall	ball	rainfall

Related Words

pack	packs	packed	packing	unpacked
migrate	migration	immigrate	immigration	immigrant
relative	related	unrelated	relation	relationship
ship	shipped	shipping	shipment	shipments
interest	interests	interested	interesting	uninteresting

High-Frequency Tricky Words

what	were	your	said	there
said	what	were	there	your
were	there	what	your	said
your	said	there	what	were
there	your	said	were	what

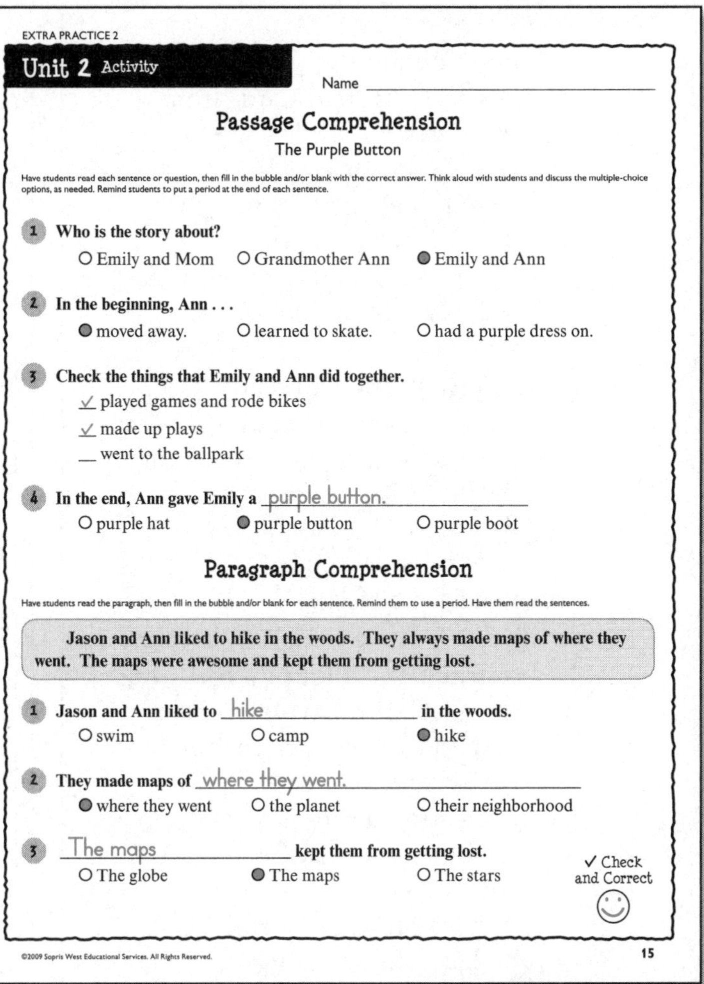

EXTRA PRACTICE 2

Unit 2 Activity

Name ______

Passage Comprehension

The Purple Button

Have students read each sentence or question, then fill in the bubble and/or blank with the correct answer. Think aloud with students and discuss the multiple-choice options, as needed. Remind students to put a period at the end of each sentence.

1. Who is the story about?
   - ○ Emily and Mom ○ Grandmother Ann ● Emily and Ann
2. In the beginning, Ann . . .
   - ● moved away. ○ learned to skate. ○ had a purple dress on.
3. Check the things that Emily and Ann did together.
   - ✓ played games and rode bikes
   - ✓ made up plays
   - __ went to the ballpark
4. In the end, Ann gave Emily a purple button.
   - ○ purple hat ● purple button ○ purple boot

Paragraph Comprehension

Have students read the paragraph, then fill in the bubble and/or blank for each sentence. Remind them to use a period. Have them read the sentences.

Jason and Ann liked to hike in the woods. They always made maps of where they went. The maps were awesome and kept them from getting lost.

1. Jason and Ann liked to hike in the woods.
   - ○ swim ○ camp ● hike
2. They made maps of where they went.
   - ● where they went ○ the planet ○ their neighborhood
3. The maps kept them from getting lost.
   - ○ The globe ● The maps ○ The stars

✓ Check and Correct

 15

PROCEDURES

For each step, demonstrate and guide practice, as needed. Then have students complete the page independently.

1. Activity

Passage Comprehension

- Have students read each sentence or phrase, then fill in the bubble and/or blank with the correct answer.
- Think aloud with students and discuss the multiple-choice options, as needed.
- Remind students to put a period at the end of sentences.

Paragraph Comprehension

- Have students read the paragraph.
- Have students read each numbered sentence or phrase, then fill in the bubble and/or blank. Remind them to end sentences with a period, where needed.
- Have students read the completed sentences.

Self-monitoring

Have students read and check their work, then draw a happy face in the Check and Correct circle.

2. Word Fluency (BLMs are located on the CD.)

- To build fluency, have students read Rhyming Words, Related Words, and High-Frequency Tricky Words. Have students read each section three times in a row.
- To build accuracy, have students read all sets with partners.

ACCURACY BEFORE FLUENCY

Word Fluency is designed to build accuracy and fluency. Students should practice for accuracy before working on fluency.

PROCEDURES

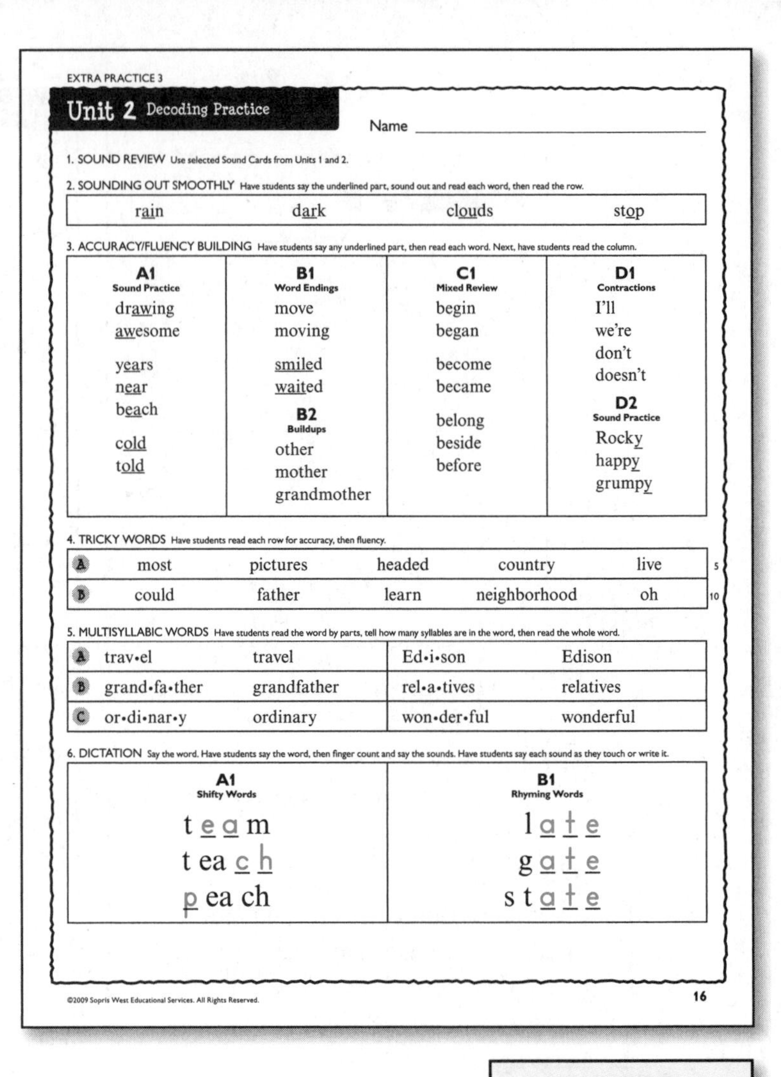

EXTRA PRACTICE 3

Unit 2 Decoding Practice

Name ____________________

1. SOUND REVIEW Use selected Sound Cards from Units 1 and 2.

2. SOUNDING OUT SMOOTHLY Have students say the underlined part, sound out and read each word, then read the row.

rain	dark	clouds	stop

3. ACCURACY/FLUENCY BUILDING Have students say any underlined part, then read each word. Next, have students read the column.

A1 Sound Practice	B1 Word Endings	C1 Mixed Review	D1 Contractions
drawing awesome years near beach cold told	move moving smiled waited **B2** Buildups other mother grandmother	begin began become became belong beside before	I'll we're don't doesn't **D2** Sound Practice Rocky happy grumpy

4. TRICKY WORDS Have students read each row for accuracy, then fluency.

A	most	pictures	headed	country	live	5
B	could	father	learn	neighborhood	oh	10

5. MULTISYLLABIC WORDS Have students read the word by parts, tell how many syllables are in the word, then read the whole word.

A	trav•el	travel	Ed•i•son	Edison
B	grand•fa•ther	grandfather	rel•a•tives	relatives
C	or•di•nar•y	ordinary	won•der•ful	wonderful

6. DICTATION Say the word. Have students say the word, then finger count and say the sounds. Have students say each sound as they touch or write it.

A1 Shifty Words	B1 Rhyming Words
t ea m	l a t e
t ea c h	g a t e
p ea ch	s t a t e

16

1. Sound Review

Use selected Sound Cards from Units 1 and 2.

- Have students say each sound, building accuracy first, then fluency.
- Mix group and individual turns, independent of your voice.

2. Sounding Out Smoothly

- For each word, have students say the underlined part, sound out the word smoothly, then read the whole word. (Use the words in sentences, as needed.)
- Repeat practice.

3. Accuracy and Fluency Building

- For each task, have students say any underlined part, then read each word.
- Set a pace. Then have students read the whole words in each task and column.
- Provide repeated practice, building accuracy first, then fluency.

4. Tricky Words

Have students read each row for accuracy, then fluency.

5. Multisyllabic Words

For each word, have students read each syllable out loud, finger count the syllables, then tell how many syllables are in the word. If needed, use the word in a sentence. Have students read the whole word.

6. Dictation

team, teach, peach, late, gate, state

- Say "team." Have students say the word. Guide students as they finger count and say the sounds. Have students touch or write the sounds, then read the word. Say something like:

  The first word is ***team.*** Say the word. (team) Say and count the sounds in ***team*** with me.
  Hold up one finger for each sound. /t/•/ēēē/•/mmm/ How many sounds? (three)
  What's the first sound? (/t/) Touch under /t/.
  What's the next sound? (/ēēē/) Write /ēēē/ with the e-a pattern.
  What's the last sound? (/mmm/) Touch under /mmm/. Read the word. (team)

- Repeat with "teach" and "peach."
- Continue with the rhyming words: late, gate, state.

CAUTION

Your children may not need Extra Practice. Use assessment results to determine if Extra Practice is needed.

PROCEDURES

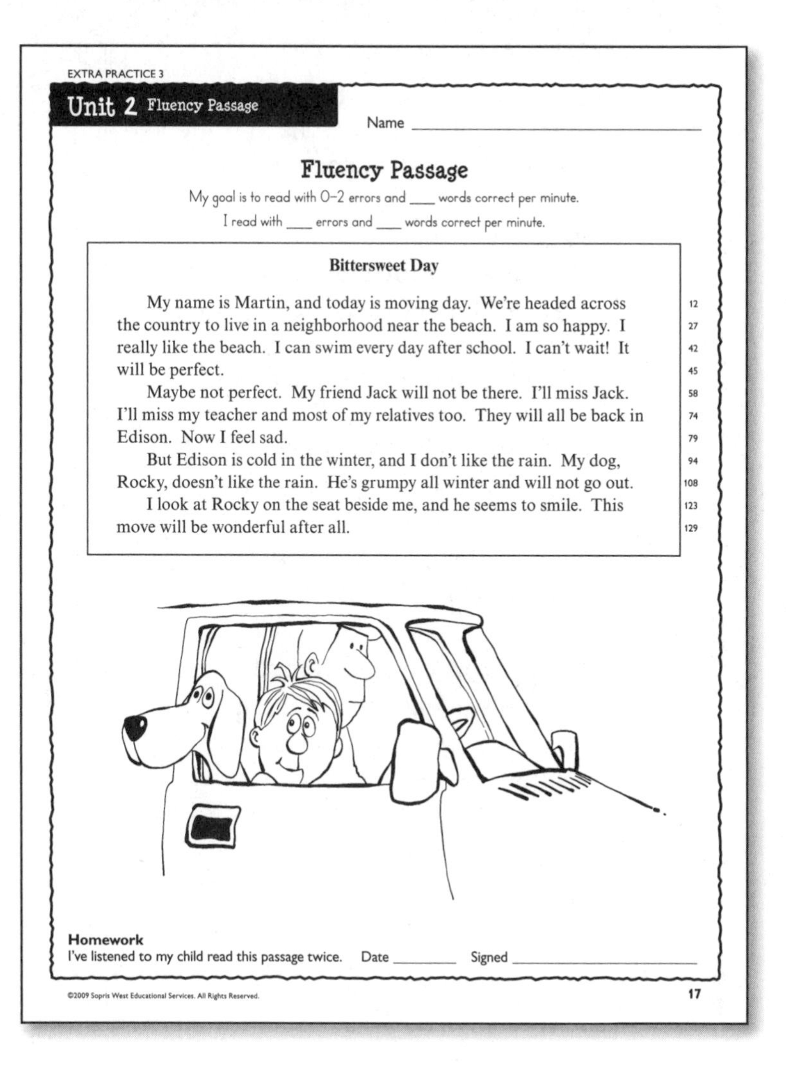

EXTRA PRACTICE 3

Unit 2 Fluency Passage

Name ______________________

Fluency Passage

My goal is to read with 0–2 errors and ___ words correct per minute.

I read with ___ errors and ___ words correct per minute.

Bittersweet Day

My name is Martin, and today is moving day. We're headed across	12
the country to live in a neighborhood near the beach. I am so happy. I	27
really like the beach. I can swim every day after school. I can't wait! It	42
will be perfect.	45
Maybe not perfect. My friend Jack will not be there. I'll miss Jack.	58
I'll miss my teacher and most of my relatives too. They will all be back in	74
Edison. Now I feel sad.	79
But Edison is cold in the winter, and I don't like the rain. My dog,	94
Rocky, doesn't like the rain. He's grumpy all winter and will not go out.	108
I look at Rocky on the seat beside me, and he seems to smile. This	123
move will be wonderful after all.	129

Homework
I've listened to my child read this passage twice. Date ________ Signed ______________

17

1. **First Reading**
   Mix group and individual turns, independent of your voice. Have students work toward an accuracy goal of 0–2 errors and practice any difficult words.

2. **Second Reading, Short Passage Practice: Developing Prosody**
   - Demonstrate how to read a line or two with expression. Read at a rate slightly faster than the students' rate. Say something like:
     Listen as I read the first two sentences with expression and phrasing. I'm going to emphasize certain words and pause between sentences.

     "My name is Martin, and today is moving day. We're headed across the country to live in a neighborhood near the beach."
   - Guide practice with your voice.
     Now read the paragraph with me.
   - Provide individual turns while others track with their fingers and whisper read. Provide descriptive, positive feedback.
     [Nikitina], you read with wonderful expression!

3. **Partner Reading: Repeated Reading (Checkout Opportunity)**

   While students do Partner Reading, listen to individuals read the passage. Work on accuracy and fluency, as needed.

4. **Homework: Repeated Reading**

   Have students read the story at home.

PROCEDURES

For each step, demonstrate and guide practice, as needed. Then have students complete the page independently.

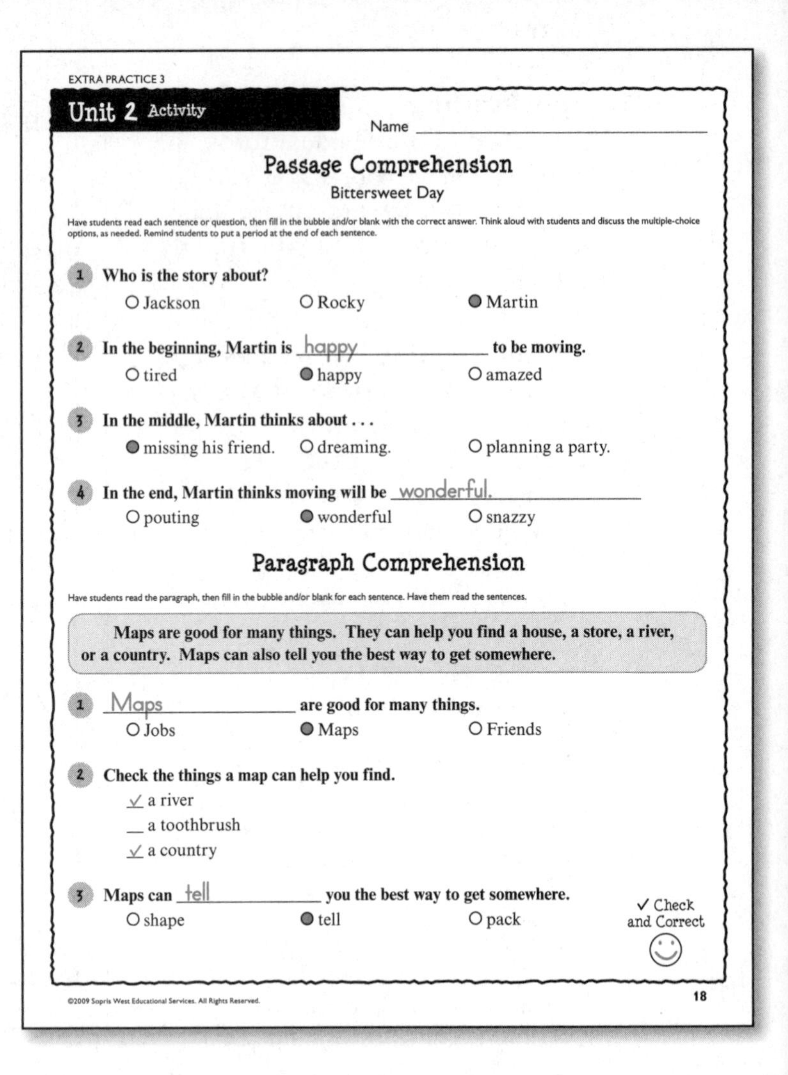

EXTRA PRACTICE 3

Unit 2 Activity

Name ______________________

Passage Comprehension

Bittersweet Day

Have students read each sentence or question, then fill in the bubble and/or blank with the correct answer. Think aloud with students and discuss the multiple-choice options, as needed. Remind students to put a period at the end of each sentence.

1. **Who is the story about?**
   O Jackson O Rocky ● Martin
2. **In the beginning, Martin is** happy **to be moving.**
   O tired ● happy O amazed
3. **In the middle, Martin thinks about . . .**
   ● missing his friend. O dreaming. O planning a party.
4. **In the end, Martin thinks moving will be** wonderful.
   O pouting ● wonderful O snazzy

Paragraph Comprehension

Have students read the paragraph, then fill in the bubble and/or blank for each sentence. Have them read the sentences.

Maps are good for many things. They can help you find a house, a store, a river, or a country. Maps can also tell you the best way to get somewhere.

1. Maps **are good for many things.**
   O Jobs ● Maps O Friends
2. **Check the things a map can help you find.**
   ✓ a river
   __ a toothbrush
   ✓ a country
3. **Maps can** tell **you the best way to get somewhere.**
   O shape ● tell O pack

✓ Check and Correct

18

1. **Activity**

   Passage Comprehension

   - Have students read each sentence or phrase, then fill in the bubble and/or blank with the correct answer.
   - Think aloud with students and discuss the multiple-choice options, as needed.
   - Remind students to put a period at the end of sentences.

   Paragraph Comprehension

   - Have students read the paragraph.
   - Have students read each numbered sentence or phrase, then fill in the bubble and/or blank. Remind them to end sentences with a period, where needed.
   - Have students read the completed sentences.

   Self-monitoring

   Have students read and check their work, then draw a happy face in the Check and Correct circle.

2. **Word Fluency (BLMs are located on the CD.)**

   You may wish to have students practice with Unit 2 Extra Practice, Word Fluency A or B.